Car~

I made a
lot of wrong
turns. I
wrote this book
so you don't have to.

Sara
♡ Clau~

He Wasn't It Either

A Single Woman's
Memoir of Lessons Learned

Iantha Ussin

Updated Version

DEDICATION

Pastor Jerry L. Baldwin, God used you, Mrs. Baldwin, and the New Living Word Ministry to walk me out of darkness into His light. Thank you for your obedience in sitting at His feet and studying His word to teach it with authority. My passion for studying the scriptures was birthed under your tutelage, and my faith walk was fueled by simply watching and emulating yours. I will always credit my instantaneous growth in Christ to the years I spent in the NLWM family under your leadership. Because of what was poured into my life there, I am able to boldly share God's truth with women everywhere.

This book, Pastor B, is for you.

The four summers I committed to *Kids Across America* in the beautiful Missouri mountains radically changed the course of my life. There, I learned to share Jesus Christ with others and led many children into relationship with Him. There, I was equipped with the tools I needed to not only study the scriptures, but also to walk them out. There, I experienced the power of God's healing. For the first time, there, I experienced God speaking to me and giving me clear direction for my life. I'm grateful to you, KAA (U KNOW!), for your obedience in creating a space for young adults to be trained for ministry. I am one of many who has taken that training into all the earth. This book is a tangible manifestation, and it is for you.

CONTENTS

INTRODUCTION

Writing this book was a fight.

A six-year fight.

More than once, I put the writing down for months at a time because I needed to revisit the moments and experiences and places that I share in the pages to come. Albeit reluctantly on most occasions, I packed up my mental and emotional bags and took a few different trips through my past. I wouldn't have been able to write without them.

Taking time away from the writing gave me a chance to reflect and rest joyfully in the fond memories from my relationships. When I remembered the good times, I found myself, at a mere thought, laughing hysterically and wearing a reminiscent smile for hours on end. I held on as long as I could, remembering every detail and reliving every moment.

Then I faced the hurtful memories, the ones that I had kept tucked away in the secret corners of my heart. I uncovered things that I'd trained my mind to forget and experienced them all again for what seemed like the first time. It was not at all like the replay of the fond memories. There were no laughs. There were no smiles. Every visitation was uncomfortable. The replays hurt. A lot. And I cried. A lot. Sometimes for days. At a mere thought.

I wanted to go back in time and change things. I wanted to reach out to a couple of the guys who live on the pages of this book. I wanted to repeat *"I'm sorry"* to them again, and with one or two of the others, I wanted to ask *"Why?"* I experienced all the highs and lows of every emotion imaginable, and in experiencing them, sometimes that meant not even being able to write.

A six-year fight.

Several times, when I got to what I thought was the end of the book, after all my trips back in time, and after navigating through all of my emotions, I realized there was more to be written. I realized I needed to give myself over to complete transparency so I could tell my story in a way that would resonate with you, the woman God told me to write this book for in the first place. But I still tried to forget that there was more to be written. I hid from the continual nagging pull at my spirit that would urge me to finish, so inevitably, procrastination became my companion. When it was time to write, I would get hungry. I would get sleepy. I would all of a sudden want to grade the papers that I'd been putting off. I would want to watch TV. I was running from the finish, and eventually, even the desire to write went dormant.

I wanted to quit.

Shoot… I *did* quit.

But then I pulled myself together and got back in the fight.

For you.

You see, there was never a doubt in my mind that God told me to write this book. I *knew* He wanted me to write it. For you. You have always been my "why"—the reason I pushed past and prayed through all the discouragement and fear I faced while wallowing in those waves of procrastination. Every time I thought, *"Who's even gonna read this?"* I prayed and pushed past it. When I found myself saying, *"Girl, you did some dumb stuff, and your 'dumb girl' moments were reeeaal dumb,"* I prayed and pushed past it. When the *"What are people gonna think?"* tune played over and over in my mind, I prayed and pushed past it.

For you. My "why".

Because my life is not my own.

I knew I would have to expose pieces of my life's journey that no one knows, but I also knew if you, the woman God told me to

2

write the book for, could learn from those pieces, my transparency wouldn't be in vain. The Lord assured me that my story will remind some women, and teach others, that their worth is in Him and Him alone. He assured me that my wrong turns and bad decisions weren't all for naught. They had purpose, and their purpose was for this time, specifically for you. I believe, with my whole heart, that I experienced all of my relationships for the sake of this moment—to share the lessons I learned with you. I am boldly confident that you will walk away from this read with the tools you need to make wise decisions in your love relationships.

Now, you may have already gathered that I'm a Christian. Jesus Christ saved my life and kept me from ruining it in my relationships. I love Him with everything in me. If you don't profess Christianity, don't let that be the reason you close this book. If you close it, you may miss the opportunity to learn from what I have yet to share. As I tell my story, yes, you'll hear all about what God taught me. You'll hear how He gave me the grace to walk through everything I walked through, but you'll also hear raw life. I talk about a relationship I had before I came to know Jesus, and I talk about relationships I had after I placed my life in His hands. I don't hide the details about the days I struggled with being in relationship with Jesus because I was more focused on the relationship with my boyfriend, and quite frankly, wanted the relationship with my boyfriend more than I wanted the relationship with Jesus. It's all here. You'll hear me address Christian women, but my story isn't just for them. My story is for any woman who has the ability to read it.

I'm sure, no matter where you stand in Christ—if you know Him or not—this book is for you. Don't miss out because of who's speaking or because of what she believes. There's something here for every woman. And even if what's here is only for one woman...

Is she you?

He Wasn't It Either is a recapitulation of Iantha Ussin's personal relationship experiences, according to her recollection and perspective, written to shed light on the lessons she learned while in those relationships. Although all of the stories are true, some names and identifying details have been changed to protect the privacy of those involved.

Puppy Love

Our eyes were too young to see that we wouldn't last, our hearts too naïve to know we couldn't...

...so along for the ride we went.

I had boyfriends throughout junior high and high school, but the relationships were never anything serious. We would talk on the phone, go to school dances together, walk each other to class, wear each other's jewelry—you know, the cutesy boyfriend-girlfriend stuff. We would greet each other and part ways with long hugs that expressed our exclusivity to onlookers, and in a few of those relationships, kisses would accompany the hugs. Sex, though, was a "no go" for me because of the examples I had from friends and family who were having sex. I could do without the unnecessary emotional drama my friends experienced that would, without fail, completely dominate our conversations and overshadow what had always been light-hearted, frivolous girl time. I could do without the fear of possibly contracting some incurable sexually transmitted disease, and I could certainly live life without pregnancy scares and earnestly having to pray for "Aunt Flow" to make her appearance. I didn't want to walk down that road.

I had plans, and the one thing that scared the breath out of my lungs, more than anything, was the possibility of getting pregnant and having a baby at that age and stage in my life. I wasn't going to be that girl. Not me. Not in junior high or high school where who you befriended and what you did with those friends was more important than who you were as an individual. I didn't want my reputation making decisions for me, which was all too common at my high school where people knew more about your sex life than they knew about you *(I still sometimes can't believe people had sex lives in high school)*. Rumors (or quiet tellings of the truth) were relentless in the hallways, too often becoming primary factors for determining one's interaction with another. And I was no stranger to measuring potential friendships against what I'd heard. I was a willing participant in the unspoken segregational code. Be friends with one of the alleged school "hot girls" and be considered a "hot girl" right along with her because I'm her friend? No thanks.

I wanted to build my own reputation; I wasn't about to allow myself to be "guilty by association".

There was no escaping all the talk about sex, though, because pretty much all of my friends were "doing it". But their "doing it" didn't affect me. My mind was made up, and my friends knew they wouldn't be getting any sex stories from Iantha. I didn't even entertain the thought of it until my high school sweetheart—my *Puppy Love*.

Butterflies

It all started that last week of our junior year because he liked me and I liked him, and back then, that's all it took. I don't remember who liked who first, but what I do recall is sitting in the hallway right outside the cheerleading sponsor's classroom door one day with some fellow cheerleaders and a few other members of the junior class who were waiting to be picked up from after-school activities. *Puppy Love* was a part of that crew. The cheerleaders were preparing for summer cheer camp and had just gotten a shipment of uniforms, shoes, pom poms, and other camp supplies. I was vigorously working on fluffing one of my pom poms because they came packaged flat, and somehow *Puppy Love* had gotten ahold of the other. The few boys who were in the hallway with us that day got quite a kick out of our girly cheerleading paraphernalia, but I don't remember *Puppy Love* taking part in much of the banter. His attention was on me. His flirty eyes would shift every now and then from me to the others in an attempt not to stare, but there were undeniable moments between just him and me, when the voices around us would seemingly fall silent, and all we would see was each other. The whole time the crew had been in the hallway, *Puppy Love* and I were a considerable distance from one another in the loose circle we'd formed, but eventually, somehow, he ended up next to me, fluffing one pom pom while I fluffed the other. Somewhere in that time when we were sitting shoulder to shoulder, there was a quiet conversation between just us. Small talk. Shy talk. Smiling uncontrollably talk. "Are you thinking what I'm thinking" talk. Somewhere in that time, we exchanged numbers, triggering a fireworks show in the pit of my stomach. And somewhere in one of the phone conversations that followed, he became my boyfriend—my *Puppy Love*.

There are guys who some girls fawn over and find good-looking that other girls don't think are attractive. And then there are guys who are without-a-doubt handsome. That was *Puppy Love*. He was good-looking, and every girl thought so. And you'd think that would make him conceited and cocky, but it didn't. And he wasn't. He was reserved. He didn't say much or offer many words even when prompted. At least not until he was comfortable with whoever was doing the prompting. Even in his circle of friends, who I could tell gravitated to him because of his cool nature, he wasn't boisterous. It wasn't unusual to see *Puppy Love* standing around with the guys, him in complete silence and the others wildly joking and jiving. He would laugh with them and be fully engaged, but even in that, he was laid back. Always watchful. Always pretty chill. He had a childlike smile that caused his small, shy eyes to squint almost to closing, and he smiled that smile often. It was warm and welcoming and made him likeable. He was always well-groomed and effortlessly well-dressed, clothed in the latest of everything. Topping off his good looks and good taste in clothing was his "good hair" and good well-to-do family, and all of that—all that "good"—is what mattered most in our high school eyes. It didn't take much at all to become boyfriend and girlfriend. For us, and pretty much every other couple, it was, I liked his "good" and he liked my "good," and just like that, in an "if you like me, check yes or no" type of way, we instantly became a match made in heaven.

Officially Official

Once *Puppy Love* and I were official, we were always together. Always. If you saw one of us, you saw the other. We'd meet up at school every morning in the cafeteria where students were required to wait until classes started. Without question, we would walk to class together, and before the warning bell rang and classes actually started, we would savor those last moments with each other in the hallway with hugs and kisses and secret exchanges that only he and I understood—our own words, our own jokes, our own love language. Then, we'd end up together at lunch after having been separated throughout the early part of the day with our very different class schedules. We'd make it our business to be together at the end of the school day too, even if I had to scramble to get changed to make it to cheerleading practice on time. I would spend countless hours at his family's house with him, and he would spend just as much time with me at mine. Most of that time, we did nothing but watch TV. Literally. There were times when we said nothing to each other; we just watched TV; we were just there. I remember working on homework and projects while he watched TV. I remember talking on the phone with friends while he watched TV, and sometimes he'd take a call while I watched TV. I even remember taking naps while he watched TV. We were just aimlessly filling each other's space. And I assumed that's how relationships were supposed to be. My sister and my female cousins seemed to spend most of their time with their boyfriends. It appeared to be that way with my friends and the other girls at school too.

Then there was the music we consumed and the movies and TV shows we watched. Song lyrics and scenes on screen were heavily ladened with a universal theme—if you're in a relationship, or if y'all are together, y'all should be *to-gether*. And those messages, of course, were inundated with sexual innuendos. I, like every other teenager I knew, was inadvertently enrolled in the "Boot Camp for Wrong Learned Behavior". I was simply playing out what I gathered from my surroundings and my association with others, thinking that what we were doing was the norm in every love relationship. I wouldn't realize until much later how dangerous all of that was and how it shaped my thinking and set the stage for the way I would behave as time progressed.

Puppy Love was already a licensed driver at the start of our relationship, so whenever he had his parents' car, we'd go out to the movies, a school dance, or to chill with friends. There were even some mornings when he picked me up from home for school, and some afternoons when he drove me home from school. We were together so much that my friends, I later discovered, just decided to stop asking me to hang out. They assumed I'd be with *Puppy Love* so they didn't even bother. They certainly wouldn't have been wrong in their assumptions.

In the early days of our relationship, things were pretty light between us. Then, as time went on and we'd been together for a while, instead of us sitting on the couch watching TV as we were accustomed to, the TV would be watching us because we'd be doing more kissing than anything. Sometimes, after a date, when *Puppy Love* would drive me home, we would sit in the car for a spell before getting out, and we'd make out. The kissing eventually led to touching, and the touching led to feeling, and before we knew it, that whole scene became routine. Pretty much every time we were together, we were *together*.

And the weekends were a given. If I wasn't doing something with my family, I was with *Puppy Love*, and if he wasn't with his family, he was with me. If I had plans to hang out with my friends, I would make sure those plans didn't consume my entire day because there had to be time for me to be with him. Likewise, *Puppy Love* made sure the time he spent with his friends didn't spill over into our time. When I had cheerleading practice on the weekends during competition season, I would try to arrange for him to be the one to pick me up after practice. It became so second nature for us to be together that we unknowingly shut everyone else out. We were each other's appendages, joined at the hip, bubbled in our own world.

Sometimes we'd be on the phone and hardly even talk to each other. We had some dialogue, of course, but even when we realized we had nothing more to say, we would just hold on to the phone. I remember times when I wanted to end a call so I could do other things, but there was an inexplainable magnetic pull between us, with Krazy Glue strength, bolting me in place and holding him right there with me. My 17- and 18-year-old life had become him. I was too involved. *We* were too involved, and that—the constant togetherness—without a doubt, was dangerous. We would find out soon enough.

Throughout senior year, and especially as it got closer to the day I was scheduled to leave for college, my dad would share little nuggets of wisdom with me about college life. He told me how to best handle my finances. He talked to me about the realities of going from having my own room to having a roommate. We talked about how my friendships would change and that that was okay. He covered it all! More than anything, though, he stressed the need for me to detach from things of old so I could embrace the new. Without his directly saying so, I knew what he meant. I knew he wanted me to start my new chapter in life without that Krazy Glue attachment to *Puppy Love*. He didn't want me to be concerned about what was happening with *Puppy Love* at home while I was away trying to focus on school. Ultimately, he would leave me to make my own choice, but he was sure to let me know how things could turn out if I decided to hang on. My dad had never steered me wrong, and I trusted his wisdom, so after processing everything he shared, I initiated a couple of conversations with *Puppy Love* to try to convince him that we shouldn't even try to stay together. I told him it just wasn't realistic to think we'd make it. But the talks didn't end in my favor. Instead, they pulled on my heart strings. So, somewhat reluctantly, I decided to stay with *Puppy Love* because he thought we could make it work even though I was going five hours away to Louisiana Tech University and he would be staying home in New Orleans to attend a local university.

Because I'd done a month-long summer program at Tech to earn college credit right before starting my senior year of high school, I knew what was about to happen when I got to Tech that fall. And it did. I was thrown into a new, demanding schedule that was nothing but class, study, make new friends, figure out who I was going to be and what I would be involved in on campus, and then repeat that, and repeat it again. "Miss Independent Iantha" was working on establishing the same Homecoming Queen status on Tech's campus that she'd had in high school, and *Puppy Love* had nothing to do with that new Iantha. The Louisiana Tech Iantha was about to be nothing like he'd known.

Seasons Change

As my first quarter at Tech progressed, I watched every one of my dad's words play out right before my eyes. *Puppy Love* and I talked on the phone less and less, I thought about him less and less, and I didn't care anymore about making us work because I didn't think it was a good idea to stay together in the first place. Naturally, being five hours and hundreds of miles apart, how often would we be able to see each other? Certainly not as much as we'd been in the habit of, that was for sure. I saw *Puppy Love* back home on whatever breaks I took that freshman year, and those breaks were very few, but there is one time I saw him that was pivotal for me. It will forever stand as the defining moment that taught me what I want and what I must have in a man.

It was hurricane season 1998, and for the city of New Orleans, hurricane season means **prepare**. Many families ready themselves to stay in the city and weather the storm because quite a few hurricane scares result in nothing but heavy rain and winds and flooding. Every year, however, some storms are expected to be more dangerous than others (and are), and families have to decide if they'll stay and stick it out or leave the city for higher, dryer ground. For this particular hurricane, sometime in September that year, *Puppy Love's* family believed it'd be best to leave New Orleans. Meteorologists were following the hurricane's path very closely, and it was projected to be a big one. *Puppy Love's* family decided to travel north and set up camp 30 miles from Louisiana Tech in Monroe, Louisiana. His family thought nothing of driving the extra 30 miles so they could see me and, of course, so *Puppy Love* and I could have some time together. His parents took us all out to eat. Then, along with one of my friends, I showed them around campus, highlighting all the places that were particularly important to me and my early campus involvement. After the touring was all said and done and we'd circled back to my dorm, his parents bid us farewell and headed back to Monroe. *Puppy Love* would spend more time with me, and I would later drive him back to Monroe. That day was the first time that sex ever seriously crossed my mind, and it was in the most unemotional, disconnected, matter-of-fact way.

Danger Ahead

I believe both of us were thinking that just because we had the opportunity to do whatever we wanted, we definitely should. I mean, his parents *did* leave us together with nothing but time and opportunity, right? Maybe they even expected that that's what would happen. Although I wasn't as into *Puppy Love* as I once was, and I didn't feel as close to him as I once had, the moment was there. I tried to conjure a sense of "pick up where we left off," and even though he felt like every bit a stranger, I still reached deep for emotions that were held up in storage. I attempted to tap into feelings that were on reserve from all that time we'd spent together before, but in that moment, in the core of my being, I had no true desire to give of myself to *Puppy Love*. My mind began to reason, however, that this was what was supposed to happen, even if it wasn't what I really wanted. Our relationship had already seen hot and heavy kissing, and we weren't strangers to feeling all over each other, so why not just "go there"? I began to rationalize.

His family made the extra effort, and I know he wanted to see me, so if for nothing else, for that, I should.

The thoughts were racing through my mind in a continuous stream.

Let me just go ahead and get it over with. Yeah, I'm scared, but it's come to this. It's about time anyway.

I distinctly remember being the first to verbalize that we should have sex, and I remember anxiously awaiting his response as we carried on with other things throughout the day. My mind kept rehearsing.

The sooner we start, the sooner it'll be over.

That was my thinking. Emotionless. Indifferent. It was mindlessly robotic. Careless, even.

As time wore on, we mentioned sex once or twice. Then, at some point, there was less talk between us, and I started executing that learned behavior—what I thought was normal because of what I'd seen on TV and heard in music, and from what I'd observed of my friends and family, even though it didn't *feel* normal in my heart. I turned on some mood music. I dimmed the lights. I set the atmosphere for sex, having no clue from any first-hand experience what that even was. But because *Puppy Love* and I had already created a pattern of aimless togetherness—just being together for togetherness's sake—it was nothing for us to "just be together" in that moment. Again, in my heart, it may have felt foreign, but in my physical body, it was just like brushing my teeth. Routine.

And there was the danger.

HE WASN'T IT EITHER

It wasn't the moment that sex was about to happen that things got risky; it was everything we'd done before that made the moment dangerous. We had been planting seeds a little over a year prior to that moment, and those seeds had grown with time and were now in full bloom. We knew all too well, from our seed stage, how to physically relate to each other, and just like a seed doesn't have to be told how to grow, we didn't have to be told either. We just grew right into our next stage of danger.

The mood was set. First, the familiar kissing. Then, the familiar touching and feeling. Then, a moment we had never seen before, one that caused me to squeeze my eyes shut and hold my breath. We were closer than we'd ever been to what my friends and the music and movies had detailed as a moment of shock and momentary pain. I waited for it, but before I would experience what I'd built up like a sky-high mountain in my mind, there was a sudden pause in our stirring. With my eyelids still nervously glued together, I felt *Puppy Love* shift his weight and sit up on the bed. Curious about what had happened to the progression of our pending "Danger Finale," I slowly opened my eyes and found that his eyes had already been waiting to meet mine. Nothing had happened, and in that moment, with very few words, we decided that nothing would.

Who knows? Maybe *Puppy Love* was thinking that my roommate would pop up, even though I'd assured him she was gone for the weekend as she had been every weekend since the start of the school year. Maybe it was the drab lifelessness of the dorm room. Or was it how unusually nervous I was with him in that moment, so nervous that I couldn't even keep my eyes open? He could have maybe even been feeling the same distance from me that I had felt from him. He could have been going through the motions just as I was in that moment. Who knows if it was both of our hearts just knowing that it wasn't right for us? Whatever the case, all I can say is: *I thank God for His protection over my life!*

I thank God He saw through my carelessness in that moment and knew that in the depth of my heart, I had no desire to have sex. That wasn't His desire for me either. God knew the plans He had for me. He knew that I still had to meet Him later that school year and give Him my whole heart when I would later get saved at a women's Bible study. He knew I hadn't even begun to understand what love is because I hadn't yet met Him. He was going to show me that my time with *Puppy Love* was exactly that—puppy love. He was going to show me that puppy love is fleeting, but His love is everlasting. He was going to show me that He'd paid a price for my body, and He would teach me that it was designed to be given only to my husband in marriage.[1] He was going to remind me that sex wasn't some random act of boredom or happenstance, or even a decision to be carelessly made by two people who'd simply been together for a long time. He would teach me that sex was a covenant designed for procreation and to create oneness between a husband and wife. So, until he showed me, He kept me. He protected me. He shielded me in my foolishness so I could experience real love and righteous, fulfilling sex with my one-day husband.

The Beginning of the End

That day with *Puppy Love,* as I said, was pivotal. It showed me what I want and must have in a man. The eye opener was when my friend and I took his family on the campus tour. I could see that as I was showing and sharing, *Puppy Love* felt completely out of place on my campus. Yes, it's natural to feel a bit disjointed when you find yourself somewhere you've never been, but his demeanor wasn't that of someone who was visiting a place for the first time. He was aloof and seemed not the least bit concerned about the places I showed him and the stories I used to connect me to those

---

[1] I Corinthians 6:18-20, *Holy Bible*

places. His parents had great interest, but *Puppy Love* was completely devoid of any. I was quite embarrassed later, after the tour, when I had to answer my friend's questions about his distant eyes and the obvious showing of his mind being elsewhere. He had been pretty standoffish with my friend too, as if he couldn't care less about who I'd been spending most of my early college days with.

He couldn't relate to anything that was going on with me. It was clear that on-campus life was unfamiliarly uncomfortable for him, but it was home for me. So, in that moment, we instantly became estranged—aliens from different planets. *(But this was who I was about to have sex with, even after seeing that! Thank God for His protection!)*

That same friend rode with me to get *Puppy Love* back to his parents in Monroe, and she even said the silence between us in the car was a sure sign that the separation had commenced. He and I had ridden in my car together many times before and it had never felt like that. *That* time, we were two different people, though, who were clearly headed in two different directions.

That 30-mile drive was one big epiphany. I was able to think back to our relationship from its high school days and see that we didn't have much in common then, either. *What in the world were we even doing together?* I loved school and everything about it. I studied constantly and worked hard on projects. I had all Honors and AP classes senior year, and I made it my personal goal to finish them all with A's. *Puppy Love* didn't share my excitement for school, though. I'm sure he kept up with and worked on assignments because it was almost impossible to survive at our school if not, but I rarely saw him working on assignments or heard him talking about working on any.

I liked being around people, if I knew them or not. He didn't care to mingle too much with people he didn't know. In fact, when he spent time with my extended family one holiday, he was like a turtle in a shell. I found myself not spending as much time with my family that day because I was trying to cater to him and make sure he didn't feel left out. I missed out on some precious moments that day.

There were other instances I was able to point to in my mind while driving in silence to Monroe, and they all showed just how different we were. I realized that we were together because we were just together. And that's what puppy love is—I like him, and he likes me, and we don't even really know why, but we're together.

I understood college to be my next step—the major connecting piece to my future. Getting there was hard, calculated, work, and I planned to do well. I planned to graduate and be the first in my family, on my mother's side, with a college degree (*and I was*). I was beginning to learn, during freshman year, that I didn't need anyone that closely connected to me who wasn't on my path. If I was going to be with someone, it would have to be someone who thought about school as I did and valued it as much as I did. *Puppy Love* didn't see college as the connection to the next step in his life, and that was fine with me. I understood we all take different routes toward our success, but if *Puppy Love* and I were going to stay together, we needed to have similar paths. I knew if his path was different from mine, he would have to do it without me. I would have to be with someone on my planet, and he needed to be with someone on his.

After his Tech visit, there was absolutely nothing happening with us. We continued to grow more and more distant. It wasn't until the end of my freshman year at Tech in 1999 that *Puppy Love* and I completely broke it off, but I was able to say before then, during that decisive day at Tech, without a doubt…

He wasn't it.

Puppy Love in Perspective

Young love very rarely grows old.

Now, let's pause for a bit. I have to give you some background before you can understand the perspective I gained from my relationship with *Puppy Love*. Without the background, you'll miss it, so follow closely and stick with me. I'm going somewhere.

A wise man once told me that a person's last words are the words they want others to remember most. It happens in public speaking and writing all the time. When a writer or speaker is closing, they usually give the last "power punch" and sum up every important thing that was said into a bite-sized, leave-and-take-this-with-you kind of way. In the following passage of scripture, after having done all that God had sent Him to the earth to do, Jesus gives His disciples some final words before He ascends into heaven to forever sit at the right hand of God.

> *Jesus came and told his disciples, "I have been given all authority in heaven and on earth. Therefore, go and make disciples of all the nations, baptizing them in the name of the Father and the Son and the Holy Spirit. Teach these new disciples to obey all the commands I have given you. And be sure of this: I am with you always, even to the end of the age."*
>
> **Matthew 28:18-20 NLT**

Jesus left His disciples with a pretty important assignment. He commissioned (commanded) them to make disciples (believers, followers, students) in all the world, just as He, Himself, had made them. He told them to teach the new disciples everything He'd taught them and to be encouraged by knowing He would be with them as they went. In this passage, Jesus is speaking directly to His disciples of that time, but this passage, and every other one like it, is just as much for today's disciples as it was for the disciples of old. Christians, who are all made disciples by other disciples, are to go into all the earth and make more disciples. That's it. We are to teach others everything Jesus taught, and God was gracious enough to give us different gifts and talents to get it done. **Our purpose then, as Christians, is to use our gifts and talents to lead others into relationship with Jesus Christ and make them disciples.**

> *Just as each of us has one body with many members, and these members do not all have the same function, so in Christ we who are many form one body, and each member belongs to all the others. We have different gifts, according to the grace given us. If a man's gift is prophesying, let him use it in proportion to his faith. If it is serving, let him serve; if it is teaching, let him teach; if it is encouraging, let him encourage; if it is contributing to the needs of others, let him give generously; if it is leadership, let him govern diligently; if is showing mercy, let him do it cheerfully.*
>
> ***Romans 12:4-8 NIV***

> *Each one should use whatever gift he has received to serve others, faithfully administering God's grace in its various forms. If anyone speaks, he should do it as one speaking the very words of God. If anyone serves, he should do it with the strength God provides, so that in all things God may be praised through Jesus Christ. To him be the glory and the power forever and ever. Amen.*
>
> ***I Peter 4:10 NIV***

Still with me? We're almost there.

When God created us, He created us each with distinct gifts and talents. Some are created with the ability to sing; it just comes naturally for them. Some have the natural ability to play sports well *(that's definitely not me)*. Some are naturally gifted at creating—artists, composers, inventors. Most of us have multiple gifts, and no one has to teach us how to operate in those gifts. We just know what to do. Throughout our lives, as we use our gifts and talents, they develop and become stronger; people and circumstances nurture them along the way.

Let me give you an example.

I'm gifted with dance ability. No one had to teach me how to dance. Rhythm and movement just come naturally for me. As a child, I could hear music—any music—and I knew how to dance to it, no matter the tempo, tone, style or genre. I just knew what to do. I'd often watch dancers on TV and mimic what they did. I'd watch family members dance, and I'd mimic what they did. I could learn any dance move from simply watching it being done. Eventually, I'd hear music and create dance moves and entire routines on my own without any training or guidance because it was just in me. And that was all before I was old enough to understand that my dancing was a gift and that people actually enjoyed watching me dance. In elementary school, when I became a part of the McDonogh #32 Majorettes, my family and I realized that I was not only superior in dance ability, but that I was quite a choreographer too.

In every group thereafter, from elementary school through college—majorette, cheer, and dance—I was sought out to lead. I knew how to perform and make audiences "go there" with me. I was always dancing and expressing myself in movement, and that didn't change when I became a Christian. In fact, my gift of dance, by that point in my life, had reached maturity. I had the foundation I needed to do what God had created and gifted me to do—speak and teach His Word through dance and expression. This was one gift I would use, one tool, to make disciples and fulfill my kingdom-building purpose.

Now what does all of this have to do with putting my time with *Puppy Love* in perspective? It has *everything* to do with it.

Years after my relationship with *Puppy Love* ended, God showed me some things that shed light on what had happened with us, and it had everything to do with purpose. When we—*Puppy Love* and I—were together, I wasn't a Christian and I didn't know God, but that didn't mean I wasn't created on purpose, with purpose, for a purpose. Even though I didn't understand that there were specific things God created me to do, I understood that I was supposed to be working toward *something*. *Puppy Love* was created with purpose too, and even if he didn't know he was created to do a specific thing, he, too, should have been working toward *something*. But he wasn't. And that's the reason why I became so uncomfortable in the relationship. We weren't walking the same walk.

Puppy Love in Perspective #1 – If he's looking to be in a relationship with you, he should know who he is, where he's going, and what he wants.

I became frustrated and uninterested when *Puppy Love* showed no signs of what he wanted in that season of his life. I knew what I was doing, I knew what I wanted, and I knew where I was going. I also realized that if I was going to be with someone, I needed to know what he wanted and where he was going too. I was using every gift and talent God had given me, involving myself in everything my schedule could fit, but I never saw *Puppy Love* get excited about much. I never saw him take anything on as his own. Everything in me wanted to connect with someone who was going after the same things I was, and I didn't even realize it until I looked up and saw myself with someone who wasn't. *Puppy Love* and I no longer walked the same walk, so our being together was aimless. Our being together had no purpose, and that was a waste of time.

Yes, we were only just fresh out of high school and most people don't know exactly what they're going to do with their lives at that point, but I learned that if a man is not even concerned about his next step, I can't walk with him. If he doesn't have a vision and plan for himself, why would he have a vision for our relationship? He won't know where we're going, so why would I hang around to wander about with him? Why would I even connect with him at all? How would that benefit either of us? God showed me that relationships with that kind of exclusivity need purpose, whether the relationship exists when the two people are fresh out of high school at 18, or if they're nearing death at 80.

So, know this…If you're a woman of God, and God has shown you your gifts and talents and how to use them to make disciples, you'll be wholly satisfied only in a relationship with someone who understands his gifting and how to use it to make disciples. Any other relationship will be frustrating. Any other relationship will be unfruitful. Any other relationship will be a waste of time. If you're with someone who only wants to hang out and kick it and has no clue what he's doing with his life, do yourself a favor and walk away. If he hasn't connected to his disciple-making purpose, you won't be at peace in relationship with him. There's no doubt about it. This is why God warns us to steer clear of dating an unbeliever (being unequally yoked[2]); believers and unbelievers don't have the same mission. A relationship that doesn't have God's purpose as its driving force is draining and won't produce much of anything that offers true fulfillment.

Know that there should be purpose even in a man's pursuit of you. He needs a plan, an "almost plan," or even a desire/idea/dream that he hasn't quite developed into a plan yet,

---

[2] II Corinthians 6:14-15, *Holy Bible*

but knows it's from the Lord and has promise. He should know his assignment, and he should seek to determine if you can connect with the assignment. He shouldn't be seeking you out just because you're cute. He shouldn't be seeking you out because you can cook and you make good money. He shouldn't be seeking you out because he wants someone to settle down with. He should be seeking you out to connect with the assignment and plan God gave him to make disciples and build the kingdom. All of your other qualities—your looks, your cooking, and everything else you have to offer—will be the much-appreciated, favorable icing on his cake.

Puppy Love in Perspective #2 – Your gifts should be in full operation while you're single so you'll know if you connect with him in purpose.

Our gifts have to be operating while we're single. We're all created with purpose to do a specific work in the earth, and if we're not connected in purpose with a mate, we should be doing what God has given us, individually, to do. When God presents you to a man, he should find you being who God created you to be and doing what God created you to do. How else will he know if he can connect with you in purpose?

There's nothing worse than having the "I'm Waiting on My Husband" mentality. This is when a woman's focus is more on getting a husband than it is on living out the purpose for which she was created. She wakes each morning, and maybe she prays and reads God's Word. She showers and gets ready for work. After a little breakfast, she heads out to work, or she grabs breakfast on the way. She puts in a full day on the job and then heads to the gym. After her work out, she swings by the grocery store to grab a few things and then heads home. Once there, she showers, eats a light dinner, and settles in to watch a couple of her favorite shows.

Finally, she gets ready for bed and turns in for the night so she can do it all over again the next day.

Her Saturdays are for relaxing and hanging out with family and friends. She may go shopping or to a movie. She may take a road trip. She may even attend a special function at her church. On Sunday, of course, she's at church. Where else would she be? She gets extra cute for the worship service because this is the day one of the single brothers in the church might "find her". She makes sure she's on her feet whenever the praise team sings. She is extra attentive during the message, evidenced by her pages of notes. After service, she talks with some of the members she knows, and she looks through the announcements and the church calendar to see what's coming up so she can attend anything that fits in her schedule. This woman believes she's doing what God would have her do. She's not clubbing; she would never! She's not hanging out with the wrong crowd; she's cut those people from her life. She's not accepting dates from people she knows aren't worth her time.

Yes, she studies the Word, she prays, and she goes to church, but that's it. She's not doing anything intentionally purposeful to make disciples and build the kingdom. Why isn't she involved in some outreach at her church? Isn't there *something* she can be doing that will put her gifts to work to help someone else? Why isn't she doing something *outside* of church? Is there not a group, club, or organization that's set in Christian principles with the sole purpose of making disciples and building the kingdom that she can join? How does she think a man will even know if he can connect with her in purpose? For a man of God who knows his purpose, a pretty face, snatched waist, and regular church attendance won't be enough. Ebonically speaking, when he sees that you ain't doin' nothin', he gon' leave yo "do nothin'" self right there!

If you've been to any singles conferences or have sat under any teaching directed to single men and women, you've heard the story of Ruth and Boaz[3]. I honestly don't even like using the story because it's been somewhat idolized by single women *(I have my own feelings and convictions about that)*, but it *is* God's Word and we learn from *all* of God's Word, so I'll use it to make this point: **Ruth caught Boaz's attention while she was working.** That's all I will say about that here, but you can read the book of Ruth in the Bible to get the full story.

It's my heart's desire for every single Christian woman to understand that her undivided heart and service are to be dedicated to the Lord (single men too).[4] Her job is to be about His business, and although she may desire a husband, it shouldn't consume her every thought (Ruth desired a husband). It shouldn't be the reason she dresses up. It shouldn't be the reason she attends a particular church or the reason she sits on a particular row. It shouldn't be the reason she does anything she does. Her doing should be to please the Lord by making disciples and building the kingdom, and her husband should find her doing just that.

Puppy Love in Perspective #3 – *You're designed to want to give, but you don't OWE him ANYTHING.*

Just because he's done something for you, doesn't mean you're obligated to do something for him. Now, don't get me wrong. We should definitely give to one another. We're called to do that in all of our relationships. We *should be* giving. Don't hold back on showing love to someone you're dating or courting just because he's the man and you feel he should be taking care of you. That's warped thinking. Believe me, no one is more traditional and old-fashioned than I am when it comes to this. I believe a man should take care of me when he asks to have my time, but if I desire to be with him too, and if he and I have found that we're on the same

---

[3] The Book of Ruth, *Holy Bible*

[4] I Corinthians 7:34-35, *Holy Bible*

page with where the relationship is headed, I should be showing him that I can give to him and care for him as well. But I won't be giving of myself *just because* he gave to me.

So, know this…If he didn't do whatever he did for you because he genuinely wanted to, that's his fault. If he is disgruntled because he bought dinner and was expecting something and didn't get it, again, that's his fault. His thinking is wrong. Not yours. He should treat you to dinner because he wants to spend time with you. If he has to "take from you" because he gave to you, he's not worthy of you. If you feel you have to "give of yourself" to "give back to him," *your* thinking is wrong. The gift of your time and the pleasure of your company is enough, and you need to rest in that.

Women, by nature, are givers. When we're in relationship with someone, we want to shower them with love and affection, and if we're with them long enough and experience enough together, we want to seal the connection with physical intimacy and sex. We're wired that way. But we must be careful to honor God's standard for sex, and His standard is marriage.

Because sex is designed for marriage, when you have sex with someone you're not married to, your emotions get connected to the other person as if you're in a marriage. Your emotions, however, don't understand that nothing else in your relationship is sealed by the marriage covenant. When that happens, your emotions are all in, even if the relationship is not. This is unfortunate and what causes the confusion and the hurt that so many women experience in failed relationships where sex was present, and that confusion and hurt is the result of what's known as a soul tie. We can thank the hormone *oxytocin* for that.

Oxytocin is known as the love hormone. It is produced in the hypothalamus in the brain and is released during sex, childbirth, and lactation. It influences social behavior and emotions, such as bonding (like a mother to her child), relational connectivity, and the creation of memories. Studies show that females usually have higher levels than males and that the first stages of romantic attachment produce higher levels (the warm and fuzzies stages).[5] During sex, when oxytocin is released, it creates connection, and that's the type of connection that God, in all His splendor, designed for marriage. He wanted the bond between married people to be much like that between a mother and her newborn baby. That type of bond is not designed to be temporary, and the intimacy required to create it is not to be taken lightly or handled haphazardly. We shouldn't casually engage in that type of intimacy because we feel like we owe it to someone.

That day with *Puppy Love,* I had it all wrong. Not once did he ask me to have sex; I was the one who brought it up. Even if he was thinking I "owed" him sex, he didn't say it. I made moves because I felt he deserved it, but his being there with me should have been enough. The time we spent together should have been enough. The nurturing giver in me, though, wanted to give him *me.* I wanted him to have something for something, but that just isn't how God would have it. And again, I praise Him for His protection! He covered me in my ignorance and let me walk away with the lesson…for you.

Puppy Love in Perspective #4 – Bad company corrupts good character; behavior is learned.

Bad company corrupts good character.[6] I'm not saying that my friends are corrupt. Most of those friends I had in high school are still my friends today. They made their decisions and I made mine. Much of their behavior was corrupt, though, and they'd say so themselves if I let them speak in this book. We've had many "if I

---

[5] Medical News Today,
https://www.medicalnewstoday.com/articles/275795.php
[6] I Corinthians 15:33, *Holy Bible*

could do it all over again" talks over the years because they, too, recognize that they were perpetuating the cycle of what they saw being played out before them. They were having sex as a result of the sheer curiosity that formed from what was going on around us. We were drowning in wrong examples. Sex was on TV. It was in the music we listened to. Some of our parents were in shacking relationships with boyfriends/girlfriends where they were only dating but lived together and, of course, slept together as if they were married. In many of our cases, we didn't even know that sex should be reserved for marriage. In fact, the talk amongst most girls was not *if* they would lose their virginity, but *when*. It was expected. And when one did, she'd tell her friends so they'd all know about her experience. It was a cycle.

Although I was the "goodie" and scared out of my mind to give myself away, it doesn't mean those messages weren't still infiltrating my mind and being implanted into my way of thinking about sex and relationships. It doesn't mean I hadn't recorded my friends' conversations in my brain. It doesn't mean I hadn't heard the line of thinking that says, *"If you've been with a person for as long as you've been with Puppy Love, it's time."* That day with *Puppy Love*, my mind was replaying those thoughts and acting on them.

If you hear a song played over and over, it gets in your head, and when it's in your head and rehearsed, you can call it back up at any time. The same is true with the messages we have being played out before us—the ones we hear and the ones we see. If we rehearse them in our minds enough, they become a part of who we are, and just like that, we can pull them up and press "play" at any given time. This is why we have to be mindful of the company we keep. We have to be selective with what we allow into the windows of our souls—our eyes[7] (and our ears). These are

---

[7] Matthew 6:22-23, *Holy Bible*

entrances to our hearts, and God's Word tells us that we are responsible for guarding our hearts because everything that concerns us is housed there.[8]

You have to be mindful of who you allow in your space. You are what you eat, and trust me when I say it won't be long before what you're eating and the company you're keeping shows up "on" you. If the company you keep isn't pushing you toward Christ, they're pulling you away; there's no in between. I promise you, bad will influence good before good will influence bad, especially if the bad is something you're accustomed to. If you've already been heavily involved in the activity you're trying to pull yourself away from, being in the company of those who are still wrapped up in it is not healthy for you. You *will* fall. Cut the ties and find new company. It's for your own good.

Puppy Love in Perspective #5 – Do not stir up nor awaken love until it pleases (before its time). - Song of Solomon 8:4 NKJV

This verse lets me know that there is an appointed time for "love," and readers are being warned not to awaken that "love" before the appointed time. "Love," in this context, means sexual desires and any sexual behavior that encourages sexual intercourse. I had to include this warning because I know, first hand, how dangerous it can be to awaken love before its time.

Puppy Love and I went from just kissing to hot and heavy kissing. From hugging to feeling all over each other. From not even thinking about sex to almost going there, and that was only because the awakening gave way to desires, and those desires gave way to more desires. Take this, for example.

You want very badly to lose some weight and get on the right track with a healthy diet. Your personal trainer tells you that you have to cut the sweets for the first two months of your new weight-

---

[8] Proverbs 4:23, *Holy Bible*

loss training program. Every weekend, though, for about five months before your weight-loss training program began, you'd been going to Starbucks to study and write papers for class. You didn't just go to Starbucks to work either. You always had a chocolate chip cookie or a slice of banana nut bread to keep you going throughout your study session. Once you started the weight-loss training program, you went to Starbucks thinking you would be fine because you were serious about your health, and for the first couple of weekends into the new workouts and training, you ate nothing when you were there. That third week, though, you couldn't just sit there and not order a cookie, and this time, you broke down and bought not only the chocolate chip cookie, but the new chocolate chip oatmeal cookie too. This was because you constantly put yourself in front of those cookies. You awakened your taste buds, and because you put yourself in the "line of fire," you satisfied your desire.

Now that you know what the chocolate chip oatmeal cookie is all about, your taste buds are awakened and aware of it and can now develop a craving for it. This is dangerous for your diet and your weight-loss journey. Even if you're not sitting in that Starbucks, you can have a craving and want that cookie, and if you want that cookie badly enough, you will leave wherever you are to get to a Starbucks and have it. And the same is true with sexual behavior and sex itself. It takes a renewed mind and the power of God's Holy Spirit to train "love" after it's been awakened. It can be done, but I'll be the first to tell you that it's not easy. It's easier to just not awaken it at all until the appointed time.

Somewhere in the back of my mind, I thought if I wasn't going as far as having sex, I was fine. I believed I was okay because there was no way I could get pregnant or contract any diseases. And that was true, but my spirit and my purity were being compromised. Every time I kissed *Puppy Love*, it stirred up the desire for more kissing, and kissing awakened desires for other things.

Puppy Love in Perspective #6 – Have a life outside of the relationship.

I'll never forget the Monday morning one of my closest high school friends and I were talking in chemistry class. In the middle of our conversation, she pulled out some pictures that she and some of our other friends had taken at a party. I said, "When did y'all take these?"

She said, "At a party on Saturday. We had fun, girl."

It was the weirdest thing to see them all in a picture without me.

I said, "Why I ain't know about the party?"

She said, "Girl, we don't ask you to go nowhere no mo'. We know you gon' be somewhere with *Puppy Love*."

I had a mix of emotions in that moment. I couldn't even say anything. It's like a mirror was being held up before me. It was as if I was seeing myself for the first time in a long time, and I was different. I was shocked at what I saw. Her words cut me. I wasn't even being considered anymore. I had been tossed to the side, missing out on time with my friends, and I didn't even know it. In that moment, I tried to think about the last time we'd done anything together, and I honestly couldn't even remember. So, the anger I felt that was swirling in my chest for not having been considered, for not having been asked, for not having been given the chance to even say "no," was quickly blotted out by a new feeling of shame. I was embarrassed. I was "that girl" who had made her boyfriend her world. And then, after feeling the shame for a minute, I just felt sad. Was that *really* me? Sure, I had a life. I was cheerleading captain. I was in Student Council. I was in The Honor Society and doing all kinds of other stuff that my teachers suggested for me like literary rallies and writing contests. I had my family and whatever was going on with them, but I wasn't acting like it, apparently. I was involved in all those things, but I was too busy trying to either include *Puppy Love* in them or hurry and be done with my obligations so I could be with him. It was true. And in that moment, looking in the mirror my friend held up before my face, I saw it clearly. I wasn't me. I'd put me to the side so I could be "we". I lost so much time with other relationships because I was too wrapped up in the relationship with *Puppy Love*. When I asked another friend, my best friend at the time (who I was with more than any other friend), to see if she would say the same thing, she confirmed it. My heart broke all over again. *Puppy Love* and I weren't married, but we sure were acting like it, and that was a dangerous place to be. I hope this doesn't become your story.

Tweet your takeaways from *Puppy Love*.
#HWIEPuppyLove

If it resonated with you,
it can probably help someone else.

Tag me in your posts on Twitter and Instagram.

Let's connect!

@ianthasinsight

The One

You really don't want to be his/her first love.
They need to have first fallen in love with Jesus.
— TemitOpe Ibrahim

Freshman year at Louisiana Tech was an academic breeze because my college-preparatory magnet high school trained me well and actually challenged me more than my freshman year at Tech did. I was tap dancing through classes with time to spare, so I decided to seek out organizations and extra-curricular involvement that would foster my academic, social, and emotional growth. I had the opportunity to jump into a few different things, but I decided not to overextend myself as I'd done junior and senior year of high school. That meant choosing one club or organization that I could wholeheartedly dedicate my time and service to, and I decided I would do that with the gospel choir. I initially chose the choir because of my love for music and singing and to place a check by my goal of having found a place for social growth. But God used the choir as an avenue to give me the spiritual growth I didn't even know I needed, and it radically changed the course of my life.

The New Me Before "He"

Right away, I gained friendships through the choir that made my freshman year one of the best years of my life. My friends and I were always together, encouraging one another and helping each other through whatever freshman struggles we faced. I found safety in a close-knit circle of about five of us, and one of the five just happened to live next door to me in our dorm. Because we were so close physically—literally two steps from one room to the other—it was inevitable that we'd become close relationally. We got to see each other's lives up close, and I saw that she not only sang in the gospel choir as I did, but she also *lived* what we sang about. She really loved Jesus, and her love for Him caused her life to look totally different from mine. It was the kind of different that intrigued me and made me desire a life like that for myself.

Since I'd been spending so much time with my friends and with the gospel choir, I was learning things about God that I'd never even heard before. It was all so new. So real. So refreshing. I was learning what it meant to be unselfish and patient and considerate and giving, and eventually I saw myself actually being more unselfish and patient and considerate and giving. I was shedding old skin and emerging anew, and I liked it. I was breathing new air, and I wanted more of it. I was fully aware that something was happening in me. My heart was more tender than it had ever been, so it was only a matter of time before I would grab hold of the fullness of my transformation.

One night, my neighbor-friend invited me to a women's Bible study that met once a week. I had gone with her to the Bible study a couple of times before and enjoyed it each time, but that night would be different. After about an hour of studying scriptures about Jesus' death, burial, and resurrection and discussing them at length, we brought the lesson to a close. As we were closing, the leader of the study, who is one of my mentors still today, offered me the opportunity to enter into a relationship with God through Jesus Christ. The leader asked, corporately, if we knew Jesus is Lord and if we knew He lives. Then, she looked each of us in our eyes, one by one, and asked us those same questions individually. When she got to me, she excitedly asked, "Do you know Jesus lives?"

I said, "Yes!"

And she said, "How do you know it?"

"Because I believe He lives in me!" I boldly declared.

She went on to review things we'd already discussed and made sure I understood that because I confessed with my mouth that Jesus is Lord and believed in my heart that God raised Him from the dead, I was saved and in a new relationship with Jesus. I let her know I understood.

A single tear ran down my cheek. The leader embraced me. I had been singing about Jesus and learning more about Him through gospel choir Bible studies and other events, but *knowing* Him personally didn't happen for me until that night. I went back to my dorm with a fiery excitement, knowing that I'd accepted Jesus Christ as my savior and my Lord. I knew I was about to experience even more transformation, and I welcomed the change. I got plugged into a local church and committed myself to learning what it meant to live like Christ.

By the time I began my sophomore year, I had a firm grasp on who I was. I had college life completely in my grip; I knew the ropes. I was ready to start establishing a respectable, long-standing reputation on campus, so I sought out more extra-curricular opportunities. I became a Resident Assistant (RA) to a floor of mostly freshmen, and that (and later being a Hall Director) was my greatest and most rewarding responsibility as a college student. I became a University Student Recruiter because I loved my school and wanted others to attend and love it too. I was still a member of the gospel choir, Souls on Fire, but because I was a new, excited Christian, I was much more involved with the choir that year than I had been my freshman year. And as if all of that wasn't enough, I also became a member of Alpha Kappa Alpha Sorority, Inc. (AKA). My plate was officially full!

In Walks *The One*

It was February 2000 when I pledged into AKA. Shortly after becoming a member and learning what would be required of me in the sorority, our big sisters announced that they would be officially introducing us, the new pledges, to our brothers, the guys on campus who had established themselves as our co-laborers in community service. Over the years, the Louisiana Tech AKAs found solace in having brothers on campus who could help out with planning major events and assisting with executing those plans. The relationship was a treasured one. The day we met our brothers, *The One* was missing from the group. He was out of town. Apparently, he was well known on campus because some of my line sisters (pledge sisters) were able to chime in and say, "Oh yeah. That's right. He's in Arkansas. He said he won't be back until Monday." I felt like the odd ball; I had never even seen the guy.

About a week later, a few of the brothers were standing together along the main wall in the Student Center, and I was walking by en route to another destination. When I noticed a face I hadn't seen before amongst them, assuming it had to be *The One*, I knew I wouldn't be able to just wave and keep going. I knew I had to stop to meet him, especially knowing what I knew. You see, the brothers had shared with me, not long after our first official meeting, that *The One* had seen a recording of the AKAs' "coming out" pledge performance that he'd missed. Turns out, just as I'd never laid eyes on him, he'd never seen me either, but in seeing me on that video, he inquired about me. He knew pretty much everyone else on my pledge line because they were in the "in crowd," but he said there were a few of us he didn't know. He wanted, specifically, to know about me.

Mental note.

Naturally, since I knew *The One* had asked about me, I was checking him out in those first few moments. I may have even flirted a bit. He was very handsome. Athletically built. Quiet. Mysterious. Everything that was attractive to me about a man at first glance. After one of the brothers introduced us, we greeted each other with a hug and engaged in a few minutes of small talk and playful banter. Soon after, I scurried off to my next stop. Before long, I got word from the brothers, again, that *The One* wanted to know more about me.

Mental note.

Again.

Getting my phone number was not at all like finding a needle in a haystack. Since I was an RA, my phone number was published on the main floor of my dorm for emergencies. Also, back in that day, students' room phone numbers were listed in a campus directory. I reckon *The One* acquired my contact information through one of those means because I don't remember giving it to him. And just like with *Puppy Love*, I don't recall the first time we talked, or the details on how we began having regular conversations, or what was said in those early conversations, but I *do* remember wondering why I was even giving my time to someone like him. I mean, he was super popular! I didn't fraternize with that circle. I made it my business to steer clear of them because I wasn't a groupie, and although I shouldn't have, I stereotyped them and wrote them all off as jerks. I'd see girls swoon over them on campus as they readily welcomed the attention, and "that chick," I refused to be. I'd hear who was having sex with who and who was messin' around on who, and I came to loathe the conversations about the popular guys and their lifestyle. So, when *The One* and I talked on the phone those first few times, I let his talk go in one ear and out the other. I wasn't sold on him yet, and I was actually still trying to decide if I would let things take shape with another guy I'd been talking with on a regular enough basis.

Spring Break arrived, and I went home to New Orleans. While home for that week, I was receiving phone calls almost daily from both *The One* and the other guy. It had been nice getting to know the other guy because he was funny and had good conversation. I liked his laid-back nature and easygoing personality. He was in high pursuit of me, but there was nothing about him that made me want to be with him as much as it appeared he wanted to be with me. All of a sudden, I became terribly irritated with him. His behavior had become erratic and immature, and he was getting a little clingy too, so I pulled away and leaned into *The One*. I decided *The One* was who would have my time and attention. I wanted to see if things would go anywhere.

And things *did* go.

For two years.

New Butterflies

One warm, still night, not long after we'd returned to school from Spring Break, *The One* asked me to be his girl. In a "new to us" awkward embrace, I could feel his heart beating out of his chest against my cheek. His nervous arms pulled me in close and held me tight. I said "yes" with just about as much flutter in my chest as he had when he asked; it was exhilarating for us to share that jittery excitement. Although it may have been nerve-wracking for him to officially ask the question, neither he nor I had any doubt that I would respond in the affirmative. We had been enjoying our time together too much, and our being together was easy, so making it official was the natural next step. I enjoyed his pursuit of me—dinner dates, meet ups on campus just to talk, once a random rose. He knew how to woo me. And for someone who hadn't known me very long, he knew enough to know how to win me, and I was glad to be his prize.

As instinctive as it was to have made it official with *The One*, I was still really cautious with him. I didn't want to be just another somebody that another well-known guy would be able to say he'd been with on campus. I refused to have that be my reputation. It took some time for me to say to myself, and even longer to voice to others, that we were "a thing". I just wasn't ready for the public acknowledgement of the sorority girl and her "Big Man on Campus" boyfriend and all that I wasn't even sure came packaged with it, so I made him pump his brakes with me. We were definitely together, but I ensured we moved slowly.

One time, for example, early on in our dating, before we were official, *The One* wanted to visit me in my dorm well past respectable visiting hours. He'd been gone out of town for a few days and we hadn't talked much during that time, so when he returned, he figured we could talk and catch up. I wanted to talk too, so I let him visit me, but I was extremely uncomfortable with him being in my room that late. I couldn't even carry a conversation. It wasn't long before I was conjuring up a way to end our chat so I could escort him out. I didn't want to establish a late-night visit routine with him.

There were times, too, that he wanted me to accompany him to his apartment to hang out. In fact, the night he asked for us to be exclusive, we were at his apartment. But because things were still so new with us, I just couldn't get comfortable in his space. We had shared some quality time together up to that point, no doubt, but we still didn't really know each other. I wanted us to be well acquainted before we shared that kind of closeness, and I was determined to do things right. I didn't want to smother myself with him as I'd done with *Puppy Love*. I didn't want to give him any wrong impressions either, like he should expect physical intimacy with me, or like whatever he wanted, I'd bend and allow. I had to set boundaries not only to safeguard my comfort, but also because I was a young woman who was beginning to fall in love with Jesus. I was learning God's ways and how to live as a Christian, so I wanted to be sure I was honoring the Lord in how I spent time with *The One*. I later learned, as *The One* and I got closer, that those were the things that made him want to be with me even more. He liked that I'd set boundaries and took things slowly. I wasn't like anyone he'd ever been with, and the respect I had for myself was attractive. He was drawn to my standards, and it made him want to do whatever he had to do for our relationship to work.

Growth and Change

That summer after my sophomore year was a busy one. Earlier that school year, one of my brothers from the gospel choir had encouraged me to apply to work at Kids Across America (KAA), a Christian sports camp in Golden (Branson), Missouri, whose vision is to transform urban youth to impact their communities for Christ.

After he assured me I wouldn't have to play any sports or even be knowledgeable about any sports to work there, I decided to apply. I researched the camp to verify that I could serve in other capacities that had absolutely nothing to do with sports, and when it was confirmed, I applied to be a counselor. My interview went well, and I was asked to join the summer staff. Once the school year was over, I carpooled with four other students from Tech to Golden for staff training week. It was that week (11 days actually) that taught me what it really looks like to live for Christ. I would never be the same after those 11 days.

I had never seen so many young people (college students) excited about the Word of God. I knew that I was in relationship with Jesus, but I didn't know anything about showing someone else how to be in relationship with Him. I didn't know how to study God's Word, and I didn't know how to put what I'd learned into wholehearted practice. At KAA, I learned how to share my faith. I learned how to have a quiet time with God to study His Word and allow His Spirit to speak to me. I learned how to do object lessons, where I could basically use anything—nature, arts and crafts, dance, a mop and broom—*anything*—to teach someone who Jesus is and how much He loves them and wants to have a relationship with them. And I had never heard Christian music like I heard at KAA. I was a choir girl, so all I knew was choir music, but at camp, I was introduced to worship music, Christian rap, and Christian music that had the R&B flavor that I was accustomed to. I was pleasantly surprised, and I couldn't get enough. I was hungry for anything that would get me as excited about serving the Lord as everyone else was. When I saw that there was more to Christianity—that Jesus was in more places than just the church—I wanted to know all there was to know. I didn't want the training to end. The summer camp session began as soon as staff training week was over, but only for those staff members who were signed up for that first term. I was signed up for the third term, so I had to leave camp that May and return in July.

I left camp and went home to New Orleans with a fresh outlook on life. I had been trained alright! I was a new woman. I had been fed more of God's Word and seen more godly examples in those 11 days than I had since I'd been saved. I had a new thirst to know God's Word and be a godly example, so I woke every morning to study scripture for hours and learn more of who Jesus was and what He'd done.

The Chivalrous *One*

After a few weeks in New Orleans, it was time for me to go to AKA's bi-annual conference in Dallas. I would be there for a week, and that was perfect because *The One* had been in Dallas that entire summer for an internship. We hadn't seen each other since I'd left Tech in May, so I couldn't wait to lay eyes on him. *The One* had been living with family in Dallas that summer, so he was somewhat acquainted with the city. When I gave him the name and address of the hotel where I'd be staying, unbeknownst to me and without my asking, he located the hotel and checked out the surrounding area to ensure I'd be in a safe place. On the day I was to arrive, he and I spoke on the phone to discuss our plans for that day. I was planning to drive directly to my hotel, but *The One* provided me with a location for us to meet that was fairly easy to get to from the interstate and from the direction from which I'd be traveling. He didn't want me to get twisted up in the endless crisscrossing of the Dallas/Ft. Worth interstates and possibly get lost, so he had me follow him to the hotel. His plan all along was to make my transition stress free. It was such a thoughtful, chivalrous gesture.

The One was with me while I checked in. He watched the desk attendant's every move and listened to his every word. At the same time, he was like an inspector, scoping out everything in the lobby.

I watched him walk to one of the three windows that lined the wall to the left of the front desk. He looked out the window to the right, and then to the left, and then to the right again and held his gaze for a moment. Then, he turned around and walked back to where I was standing. A few seconds later, he walked back toward the windows. That time, he walked past the windows to the wall's end and peeked around the corner into what looked to be a hallway. From there, he walked back to the front entrance. He peered out the door for a moment and then made slow, calculated steps back to where I was, studying the walls to his left and right the whole way. Up to that point in our relationship, I'd seen *The One* as the pursuer who would stop at nothing to let me know he wanted to be with me. That day, it was crystal clear that he was establishing himself as my protector too. I could tell that if anything looked suspicious, unsafe, or out of place, he would spring into action. I can't say that I knew *what* he would do, but everything in me knew he wasn't letting anything happen to me. Not on his watch.

As he approached the desk, I was thanking the attendant for getting me squared away. I grabbed the room key, and *The One* and I went to my car to retrieve my things. Once we emptied the trunk, we headed to my room and spent some time catching up and reacquainting ourselves after having been apart for almost two months. It was really refreshing.

The Contrite *One*

That week, after *The One's* work days were done and I was finished with meetings, he would meet me at my hotel so we could savor every moment together. He knew he wouldn't be sleeping in my room without my even having to say it, so every night after our time together, we would bid each other adieu, and he would drive 20-30 minutes across the city to his family's house. One night, after he and I said our goodbyes and I saw him out, I began to prepare myself for bed. Just as I was about to grab my cell phone from the nightstand to return a friend's call that I'd missed, I noticed *The One* had left his pocket notebook right next to my phone. I, of course, opened the notebook and looked to see if there was anything of immediacy that he'd need for work that next day. There wasn't anything in there related to work, but there *was* a montage of women's phone numbers all over the front and back of the first page. I realized that I hadn't opened his pocket notebook, but I'd discovered his *Little Black Book*. Sure, he and I were barely four months into our "thing," but we'd made it perfectly clear with one another that we were exclusive and that we were an "us".

As I studied the names I held in my right hand, the left hand that was parked on my hip began to sweat. I could feel the blood in my veins warming up, setting the skin on my face and neck ablaze. The rhythm of my heartbeat shifted gears to a more pronounced, high-speed thumping, and I could actually feel the pounding reverberating in my ears. My breaths were coming more quickly too, and the air I pushed out through my nose felt hot. I stewed in my body's unique symphony for a time until all of its movements naturally regressed. In the anticlimactic moments that followed, when all my senses were properly realigned, I pondered my next move and eventually decided not to mention anything to *The One* right then. I expected him to call at some point that night to say he'd made it safely to his destination, but I planned to keep the conversation short. I would address the matter in person.

Conference meetings that next day were a blur. All I could think about was what I was going to say to *The One*. I couldn't wait to see him later that night so I could put that *Little Black Book* in his hand and confront every name that was connected to a phone number. I wanted to know why he felt the need to hold on to other girls' numbers if he and I were clear that we wanted only to be with each other. And that, among other things, is what I very clearly articulated in my onslaught of heated verbiage as we stood in the middle of my hotel room, face to face. I don't remember his reasons. I don't even remember anything he said, really. I just remember him, in the middle of my rant, tearing that sheet of paper up into tiny pieces and walking away from me to put every scrap into the wastebasket that sat on the floor between the two beds. Then, he plopped down on one of the beds. There was a still silence after that. In that silence, he looked up at me standing in the same spot where I'd stood for the entire ordeal, and I studied every expression on his face. I could hear his mind saying, *I just want you to trust me. It was stupid, I know, but whatever I have to do for you to trust me, I'll do it.*

I'd put him on the spot, and I let him know, loud and clear, that if we were going to be together, I was going to be it—there would be no one else. I remember telling him that I wasn't what he was used to and if what he was accustomed to was what he wanted—girls who didn't mind being one of many—we could end it right then. I refused to be one of his girls. I would be the *only* one.

We didn't have anything else to say, so that still silence simmered between us for a few minutes. I could see that he knew I meant business, hence the riddance of the phone numbers and the regret that dwelled in his eyes. The woman in me knew I could get whatever I wanted from him in that moment, but I didn't *want* anything. I *needed* honesty in our relationship, and I *needed* to be able to trust him. I *needed* us to have a mutual understanding of how "our thing" would work, and I needed him to know that having even an inkling of interest in anyone outside of *us* wasn't how it would work.

Just minutes before, I felt as if I could have been done with him in an instant, but strangely, in our silence, after all the friction had subsided, all I wanted was to be close to him. I had asked him to explain himself, and he did. I had asked him to come clean, and he did. And he had apologized sincerely. He was pitiful as he sat on the bed, and the longing in his quiet sadness begged me not to dismiss him for his mess-up. Somehow that earnest cry of his heart reached mine and wouldn't let go. The draw was strong.

I hadn't done anything to cause us pain, so I had the upper hand in that moment. Like I said, I could have surely gotten whatever I wanted right then, so it would have been the perfect opportunity for me to stand strong with my boundaries and further draw the lines that were necessary at those beginning stages in our relationship. It would have shown that I was serious about our taking things slowly, and it would have really set a firm foundation for us. I had been doing well with staying in my room alone and allowing him to honor me by driving back to his family's house every night. I was the lady that I'd always been. But then I blew it and allowed him to stay with me in my room that next night.

Opened Doors and Next Steps

The whole time *The One* was in my room that next night, I kept thinking about how awful it would be for my actions with him to have the mere appearance of evil[9]. Heck, I had considered it all that day in conference meetings; it was all I could think about. And Lord knows I couldn't get it off of my mind when I knew he was en route to me. But no matter how much the whisper of God's Word spoke to my heart, I pushed it aside and ignored it. We'd been rehearsing the same thing every night—he comes to see me, we talk and laugh, and he leaves. That night, I just wanted him to stay. I didn't want him to have to drive across Dallas because all week, I'd actually felt a little bad about it. Having him stay would make me feel better and hopefully show him that I cared about him. And I definitely felt safe and protected with him there, so there was my logic and the reasoning I allowed to trump the gentle reminder I'd received from the Lord.

---

[9] I Thessalonians 5:22, *Holy Bible*

We started the night lying in separate beds, but it wasn't long before we were cuddled up in the same bed under the guise of watching TV together. Before long, the TV was watching us, and into that night we slept.

And there it was.

Just like that, I'd started a pattern that birthed expectancy. *The One* knew there would be no sex, and he knew I wasn't the type of girl he was used to, but a door had been opened, and it wouldn't be easy to close. To him, I was saying without saying, that trust in our relationship would lead to closeness, and closeness would lead to next steps. And next steps to next steps, and...

After the conference was over in Dallas, I had a few days before I would have to head back to KAA to work my term, so I took a trip to Tech to visit some friends. *The One* took the trip with me. Our ride from Dallas to Ruston was a sort of establishing time for us, where we discussed, in detail, everything that had transpired throughout our week together. In all of it, he'd learned that I was serious about us and that I wasn't going to tolerate games and foolishness. He could see I cared about him. I'd learned that he wanted what was best for me and would go out of his way to protect and respect me. I could see he cared about me. We liked who we were becoming together. We felt secure. I knew who "we" were, and I knew where we were going. It was sealed.

I remember him saying he didn't even care what we did in Ruston once we got there, as long as we could have that day together before he had to head back to Dallas the next day. So, upon arrival, we visited some of my friends and some of our mutual friends. The rest of the day, we played by ear, together.

More Growth, More Change

When it was time for me to head back to KAA, I couldn't wait to see everyone and feel the excitement I'd felt in May. Since having left, I'd been studying and praying and doing all I knew to do to apply the things I'd learned, and when I got back in July, I learned even more. That summer, I developed in some of the foundational principles and practices that I stand firm on in my Christian faith today.

I had always known I was born to teach, but the teacher in me wasn't awakened and nurtured to life until that summer at camp. Counselors were required to teach scripted Bible studies to our campers, but it wasn't long before the Lord was teaching me in my personal study of His Word how to teach beyond the scripts. His Word was so alive in me that I just had to share more with my campers.

Counselors were also required to teach sports classes and other activities. Thankfully, as I said before, I didn't have to facilitate any sports instruction, but I did teach sailing and swimming and similar outdoor activities. I also taught a cheerleading and dance class, which was right up my alley. It was through the dance and cheer classes at KAA that I learned how to interpret God's Word with movement. Although I hadn't seen anyone dance unto the Lord before camp, it wasn't long before there was choreography pouring out of me for literally every song I heard. I would even get choreography in my dreams (and I still do). By the end of that summer, I had whole productions worked out in my head. It amazes me, still, to know that Praise Movement School of Dance, Inc. was always a part of God's plan for me. The dance school didn't come to life until five years later, but the Lord was certainly preparing me and giving me what I would need to later teach girls how to minister to others through song and dance.

That summer, for the first time, I experienced God speaking to me about things I'd shared with Him in prayer, and it would always happen when I was studying His Word. There were times, too, that I'd get entire messages (sermons) from what I read. I'd just compile the messages in my journal for personal study, not knowing that I would need some of them years later.

God taught me how to pray for the people in my life, and the most fascinating thing was learning how to pray for people at camp whom I knew only in passing and whose lives I knew nothing about. I would always know exactly what to pray for and would learn later, as our camp days went on, that what I was praying for was just what they needed.

I met people who challenged me and asked me the hard questions about my personal life and my relationship with *The One*, and one in particular was the camp's women's director. She knew I was a new Christian, and she made it her personal mission to disciple me and help me grow while I was there. In one of the many talks she and I had that summer, she asked me if *The One* was a Christian. I told her I honestly didn't know. I knew his parents were involved in their church and expected *The One* and his siblings to be involved as well, but from what I knew of him those first few months of our time together, it seemed to me that he didn't want to be involved, which made me wonder if he was in relationship with God. I understood that regular church attendance wasn't the sole telltale sign of someone's commitment to God, but I did know that when one is committed to Him, they desire to fellowship with other believers, in or outside of the church. I hadn't yet seen that with *The One*.

She asked if I could see *The One* as the spiritual leader in our relationship, and as hard as it was to reply in the negative, I told her I couldn't. There had only been a few times that he and I had talked about God and church, and those few times, I was encouraging him to go to services with me because he wasn't a part of a church.

The director and I talked about the importance of my being in relationship with someone who honored God the way I did. She helped me to see how detrimental it would be to my growth in Christ if I was with someone who only respected God rather than wholeheartedly reverenced him. And I knew it to be true. I had already experienced a bit of awkwardness with *The One* in simply asking him to accompany me to a worship service and seeing that his excitement level didn't match mine. After all of the conversation about how seemingly different *The One* and I were, my director took it a step further and asked the question that I hoped she wouldn't. She looked me square in the eyes and said, "Is your relationship pure?"

Instantly, I felt a gnawing conviction grip my heart. My eyes lowered to the step that was holding my feet, and I let that drop of my head and the silence that surrounded it serve as my answer. Even if I wanted to speak, my tongue wouldn't cooperate. It understood, too, that it wasn't required to respond.

Purity, as I'd come to understand it, was more than abstaining from sex. I knew that just because *The One* and I hadn't engaged in sexual intercourse, it didn't mean our relationship was pure. We had certainly lain together, and that, I knew, was crossing the line simply because it was opening the door to temptation and setting up unhealthy habits that would only awaken our sexual appetites. My heart broke at the thought of it. I knew I'd messed up.

For the remainder of my time at camp, I just couldn't shake the thoughts of my time in Dallas with *The One* and how I had compromised the boundaries that, albeit in place for only a short time, were very much established. I was mad at myself for being the one who'd put us in that place. *The One* did only what I invited and allowed. I wanted to honor God in every area of my life, but I felt like my relationship with *The One* was one area that didn't. I wanted to back track. I wanted to start over and stand firm, but I was afraid I couldn't because I had already activated an unhealthy cycle. And it wasn't so much my having lain with him in my hotel room in Dallas that was weighing on me. It was that I knew it was only the beginning. Even more than that was my knowing I didn't want it to stop.

To Be or Not to Be?

When camp was over in August, I was ready to get back to school and see *The One* because I missed him dearly, and he let me know every time we talked and in every letter he wrote that summer that he missed me just as much. I was jittery with excited energy as I took Exit 84 from I-20 to turn onto the Louisiana Tech University campus, but at the heart of those jitters was more nervousness than excitement. On the inside, I was crushed because I knew something *The One* didn't know—I was breaking up with him.

For days, I had been rehearsing what I thought were the perfect words, and even then, right there in my car, I was going over my lines. I had even anticipated his responses and come up with responses to those responses. I knew it would hurt him because it was hurting me. Hadn't we established just about a month ago that we wanted "us"? Hadn't he made a bold statement that declared his commitment to "us" when he scrapped those phone numbers from his *Little Black Book*? Weren't we enjoying being together? Wasn't our us-ness good? Yes, yes, yes, and yes, but I, the Iantha who'd been made new in God's presence, was deathly afraid to be in a relationship with someone who didn't want to live life out loud for the Lord. I was afraid to mess up again and establish ungodly patterns in our relationship. I was afraid to break the heart of God, and I didn't know how to not be afraid as long as I was in relationship with *The One*. I was already too wrapped up in us, and I didn't trust myself. I just wanted to end things before they got worse.

I had already called *The One* and told him to meet me at my dorm. When I pulled into the parking lot, he was there waiting for me. I parked right behind him at the loading curb and exited my car. By then, he was already walking toward me, ready to wrap me in his arms. We greeted with a hug and kiss, and I knew right then that my task was about to be more difficult than I'd anticipated.

60

Iantha Ussin

We spent the next half hour unloading my car and moving me to the sixth floor of my new dorm. With every trip we made together from the car to the building, he would hold the dorm door open and smile at me. I would smile back, naturally, but then I would have to tell myself that I wasn't supposed to be smiling. A couple of times, I redirected my attention elsewhere so I wouldn't have to. I tried, with everything in me, to keep our lovey-dovey interaction to a minimum and focus only on getting moved in, but then there were the thousands of trips we had to take in the elevator. How could we *not* talk in there? Every ascension and descension between the 6th and the main floor felt like an eternity. He talked his normal talk, and I just kept wondering if he could hear my heart beating or hear me running lines in my head. Could he see the disconnect written on my face?

We eventually got the last load into my room and sprawled out on the floor for a few minutes to recover from the move-in workout. There was some small talk and catching up, and then he went, happier than I'd ever seen him, back to his apartment. I could see that he was just thankful to have me back in town. It was crazy how I knew him so much already. He didn't hide his feelings from me; he wore them on his sleeve. His world was all right because I was in it, and I let him go home carrying that joy.

Later, once I got myself settled, I prayed and asked God to guide me in the conversation that I'd been imagining in my head all day. I knew it had to be done over the phone. I couldn't bear having done it while he was as happy as he'd been. After I prayed, I nervously dialed his number and said whatever I'd rehearsed. Those words, even though I don't remember them, were terribly difficult to utter. In fact, everything about that phone call was downright dreadful. The shivers in my speech. His incredulous silence. The questions he asked that I couldn't answer. Everything.

He was confused, just as I thought he'd be. My breaking up with him just didn't make sense, and because it was so hard to understand, it made it much more hurtful. And then there was my confusion. I, who initiated the breakup. I knew what my spirit was saying, but my mind, my will, and my emotions hadn't gotten the memo. They were tagging along for the ride and quietly following my spirit's lead, but they weren't at all in agreement. I was certain I was doing the right thing, but I was feeling like I'd written my own death sentence. Miserable was an understatement.

For hours after that phone call, I tried to continue unpacking and getting my room in order, but I couldn't. He didn't understand the breakup, and I didn't really understand either. Regret was hovering, and my longing to have *The One* in my space was fully present. What had I done?

That night, he called and called and wanted to talk and figure out what had gone wrong. He'd heard what I'd said in the break-up conversation earlier, but it just wasn't adding up. And I'd heard what I said too, but even coming from my own lips, it didn't make sense. I listened to him talk, and I responded with all the spiritual answers I could muster, trying to stand firm on what my spirit had decided, but even while I was talking, my heart was fighting to have its say. The battle was on. Even though I felt the way I felt about my growth in Christ, it was clear that I still wanted to be with *The One*. We had started something that I was enjoying, and I wasn't sure I was ready to be without him.

Needless to say, the breakup didn't last long. It probably wasn't even a week. I decided we had too good a thing going to just end it so abruptly. We could try again. We could reset boundaries. He could learn to love God. I could help him. Whatever it took, as long as I didn't have to be without him. So back into our honeymoon bliss we went.

Enjoying the Bliss, Ignoring the Miss

The One and I were growing closer every day and loving every minute together. We were respecting the boundaries that were in place—he didn't spend nights in my dorm room, even though it was allowed on weekends, and I didn't spend nights in his apartment. For the most part, we didn't keep late hours unless we were studying together, we were out on a date, or we were attending some event on campus. We both understood that we had to do things differently.

We became fond of blocking out the world around us so we could be totally locked into each other. It was our thing. We would be smack dab in the middle of Tech's crowded Student Center at high noon, when it was busiest and almost always at capacity and find a table amidst the bustle. There would be people in constant motion, talking, laughing, cussing and ranting, slamming dominoes on tables, playing loud music, and Lord knows whatever else, but we'd sit at our table and talk as if none of it was even happening. All that mattered to us was us, and we were completely tuned in.

We regularly helped each other study and complete assignments and projects. One such assignment was a family relationship questionnaire that was assigned in one of my Family and Child Studies classes. I had to pose the questions to someone I considered to be close to me, so doing the assignment with *The One* was a no-brainer. I'll never forget how that two-page questionnaire took us hours to complete because we not only answered the questions, but we delved in to discuss them at length regarding our relationship. I learned so much about him through that assignment, and he about me. I remember burying my face in a pillow and crying a couple of times throughout the process because I'd let him into a vulnerable place that I didn't even know existed. The first time I cried, I was able to recover quickly and continue with the questioning, but the second time, I needed time to regroup. When *The One* saw the state I was in, he removed all the books and notebooks that were strewn about the bed, spooned me in his arms, and comforted me. For what seemed like the most perfect eternity, he just held me and said nothing, and in that silence, I felt so close to him. Eventually, we dozed off to sleep, waking every now and then, knowing that he should leave, but not wanting to let go of the moment.

I was growing leaps and bounds in my walk with the Lord too. With my busy gospel choir schedule, the weekly Bible study where I had gotten saved, my church involvement, and my daily personal study times with the Lord, I felt like I'd become a walking Bible. Every day, I was falling more and more in love with scripture. Just as He'd done at camp, God would regularly download full sermons to me, and just like at camp, I kept them in my study journal. I wanted to share everything I was learning with *The One*, and sometimes I did, but talk about the Word of God with him was awkward, and that was painfully uncomfortable for me. He and I talked about *everything*. Nothing was ever off limits for us, but talk about spiritual things just never clicked. I always felt like I was speaking a different language.

Whenever I went to church, I went with my gospel choir friends or other Christian friends I'd made on campus. I'd invite *The One*, and he'd accompany me sometimes, but only if I asked. I remember one invitation in particular. *The One* knew I really wanted him to be there with me that Sunday. He picked me up that morning, and I could tell he'd gone out the night before. He was tired and barely made it. He managed to stay awake through the service, but he was really fighting, and I was so annoyed by that. Eventually, I got upset. And I wasn't upset because he'd gone out the night before. My mind wasn't even in that place. I was upset because I was seeing how different we were spiritually. He didn't care about the Word of God as much as I did, and I hated that we couldn't connect in that way. He had gotten up and made it to church on time in his condition, and that said a lot, but it didn't really matter because he was there only because I asked him to be. I didn't want him to be there just because I asked him. I wanted him to be there because *he* wanted to be there. I wanted to be with someone who *wanted* to live a life for Christ.

I just wanted *The One* to be able to see inside of me and understand how my innermost being had been transformed. I wanted to take him on a walking tour of my new heart and stop at every place that had been changed and explain, step by step, how it went from what it had been to what it was at present. I wanted to use diagrams and illustrations and put place markers at each stop so when he looked at me, he'd be reminded that I was new. At times, I tried to talk to him about the experiences that reshaped my spirit, but then would come the awkwardness. I could see he knew there was change in me, but he just couldn't connect to it. I wanted him to see it and feel it and understand it and, more than anything, experience it for himself.

There were many instances throughout our time together that showed me how different our lives were, spiritually, but there were other things happening, simultaneously, that brought us closer together and strengthened our bond. This— "the good outweighing the bad," if you will—is what made me fall madly in love with him.

In October that school year, my grandmother passed away. Our family knew it was coming, so I wasn't surprised, but even with the knowing, it was still a shocking blow. I was devastated. Without question, I knew I would be traveling home to New Orleans, but I knew with the way my classes were scheduled and with my responsibilities as an RA, I'd have to make a quick turnaround; I wouldn't be able to stay too long. I wanted to drive, but after talking with my parents, they convinced me that driving five hours in mourning wouldn't be a good idea. And who knew how I'd feel afterward? Would I even be able to drive back to school? I told *The One* about my grandmother's passing, but I just couldn't bring myself to ask him to drive all the way to New Orleans and be with me at a funeral for someone he didn't even know. It just felt weird. I didn't even have to ask, though, because he gladly volunteered to drive and be by my side for support. He'd already met my immediate family—mom, dad, sister and nephews—when we'd made a quick trip to New Orleans to handle some emergency business of mine, but this time, he met some extended family and was more support than I even realized I needed. For him to not only be there to comfort me, but also to take the wheel to New Orleans and back, I was forever grateful. That was one of the moments between us that helped start what I call "the love bond".

Then, in December, I attended the IMPACT Conference in Atlanta with some of my Tech friends who had worked alongside me at KAA. We carpooled there, had the time of our lives with other people from KAA, and carpooled back. It was an amazing few days. Somewhere between our leaving Atlanta and getting back to Tech, I got crazy sick. It took over me all of a sudden. I was one of the drivers on the trip, and because I was so focused on driving, I didn't realize just how sick I was. I couldn't tell, either, that driving was actually making it worse. I needed to rest. I had been on the phone with *The One* at different points throughout the drive to let him know I was exhausted and that I thought I was getting sick. On every one of those calls, he comforted me and encouraged me to get myself and the others safely back to school. When we finally arrived at Tech, *The One* was at my dorm waiting so he could get me up to my room and see about me. To his surprise (and mine), I was sicker than either of us even knew how to handle. I was a helpless mess. I had a fever. I was weak. My body ached. My head throbbed. We both thought, for sure, it was the flu.

I slept miserably that night, and *The One* slept just as miserably right there in that dorm room with me. Because I was trying my best to reset boundaries for us, he knew that sleeping in the bed with me was out of the question, but he refused to leave me.

Because I was so out of it, I didn't know until the next morning that *The One* had gotten some blankets, made a pallet, and slept on the hard, cold concrete floor next to my bed.

When he awoke from his rough slumber, *The One* saw things weren't any better with me and that I seemed only to be getting worse, so he got on the phone with my mother. I had no idea he'd called her until I woke from one of the many naps I took that day. When I was alert enough to talk, he called her again so we could both speak with her. I wasn't able to talk much, so after a few words, she just went on talking with *The One*. I heard everything. I heard her giving him detailed instructions about getting me to a doctor. I heard her telling him to monitor my temperature because I had a history of seizures that were triggered by high fever. I even heard him getting the details about what I needed to eat, even if I didn't want to. She asked if he was financially able to take care of the doctor's visit that she and my dad would immediately reimburse him for, and he said he was.

That afternoon, *The One* assisted me with getting dressed decently enough to get to Urgent Care. He talked to the doctor. He did paperwork with my mom's help. He. Did. It. All. He took care of it so well that I can't even remember the details. I remember it being confirmed that I had a sinus infection. I remember having to go to Walmart afterward to have my prescription filled and sitting in the car seemingly half dead while he took care of that too. *The One* stayed with me the next couple of days, nursing me back to health. He went to his apartment periodically to take care of himself, of course, but as much as he was able to be there with me, he was. And until I was completely able to do for myself, *The One* was my caretaker. There were countless other instances like that one that just strengthened the love bond, and strengthened the love bond, and…

Skating on Thin Ice

We were growing closer, so that meant more doors were opening for us to step outside the boundaries that I'd attempted to put in place. At that point in the relationship, our times together were drifting into late night hours. We'd gotten to the point where it just made sense to spend the night together. We'd grown weary of the routine of saying good night when it really wasn't what we wanted to do. There was no way I would let *The One* stay the night in my room because I was the RA, and I was trying my best to set an example, but if we were ever hanging out late in my dorm and we knew we wanted to continue past visiting hours, we would just mosey on over to his apartment. The uneasiness I'd felt with being in his apartment at the beginning of our relationship was no more. As time wore on, the discomfort was less and less, and falling asleep with him in his bed was anything but foreign. We would sleep for a few hours, and somewhere in the middle of the night or super early in the morning, I'd wake him so he could get me back to my dorm because technically, I was always on duty. I wasn't supposed to sleep away from my dorm unless my Hall Director was aware of it, so I was knowingly violating the laws of the land.[10]

My job was to uphold the rules and guidelines set forth by my school and the Housing Department, but I was boldly breaching them, not only putting myself in danger and jeopardizing my little college livelihood that came by way of a monthly check, but I was also putting my residents in harm's way. Suppose something had happened when I was gone and I couldn't bear witness because I wasn't on my post? I still have moments even now that I think back to that time and thank God for covering me and my girls. I know it was nothing but His grace that kept watch over us in my time of selfishness.

---

[10] Romans 13: 1-2, *Holy Bible*

I was not only defying God's Word that tells me to obey those in authority over me[11] and to do everything as unto the Lord,[12] but I was violating my body and my spirit. I had learned to put myself to the side, the spoiled brat that I was, to see that *The One* was happy. I was willing to give of myself in almost any way but sexual intercourse to keep our love bubble afloat. And that was the breakdown of our relationship. When I began to compromise our boundaries on a regular basis, I felt the Lord dealing with me, and His conviction was strong. I was beginning to idolize *The One* because I wanted him more than I wanted anything else. I loved him and loved being with him and wanted to show my love, so step by step, over time, I relaxed the boundaries. Then, they relaxed a little more. Then, they relaxed a little more until we ended up in a pattern that made my heart heavy; I knew it wasn't pleasing to the Lord. I was maintaining on the outside, but I was a tormented, confused whirlwind on the inside. I couldn't shake knowing that I was one person when I was with *The One*, and someone totally different when I was with the gospel choir or with my Christian friends. Scripture and God's love and His goodness was all I would ever talk about with them, and it was all I ever *wanted* to talk about. But when I was with *The One*, I found myself suppressing that. He and I were still good, and we were definitely enjoying each other, but I was in an internal push and pull. There was a raging war going on between my spirit and my flesh—between what I wanted, and what I knew God wanted for me.[13] There was a woman of God inside of me, screaming to emerge and live her life out loud for the Lord in *every* situation with *every* person. I wanted out of the double life. But I didn't want it bad enough. Not yet.

---

[11] Hebrews 13:17, *Holy Bible*

[12] Colossians 3:23, *Holy Bible*

[13] Romans 7:13-25, *Holy Bible*

The Love Bond

In February 2001, just a couple months after *The One* nursed me to health from the sinus infection, he and I went to New Orleans for Spring Break, which happened to fall during the Mardi Gras season. He had never been to Mardi Gras, so of course he wanted to experience it and get a good feel for what the holiday was all about. My mom, who wasn't a Christian at the time, arranged for us to have our own place while we were there. We were really playing house then. We ate dinner like a married couple. We went to bed together like a married couple. We got up and ate breakfast like a married couple. For those three or four days, we literally lived together. It was 24 hours a day, just *The One* and me, in our own place with wide open opportunity to do whatever we pleased. And naturally, with all of the time we'd spent together up to that point, and because we'd become as close as we had as a result of all we had shared, I was completely wrapped up in the moment. The opportunity to have sex was ever present, and I knew within myself, for the first time in our relationship, that I wasn't going to deny him if things began to head that way. I loved *The One*, and I was so in love with his love for me that I felt he deserved to know that love with more than my words. I wanted to share *everything* I had to give with him. And I knew my feelings were the right feelings. I understood that I was created to desire the man I loved in that way, but at the same time, I knew *The One* wasn't my husband. I knew giving myself to him would come with a price because we would be out of God's will. At that point, though, it was pretty tough to have honoring the Lord as my only reason for not having sex.

One of those New Orleans nights, *The One* was in "our bathroom" getting ready to cut his hair. He'd been experimenting with a new look for a few months and we were both loving it. To maintain that well-groomed look, however, it required him to cut his hair pretty regularly, sometimes even twice a week. I'd watched *The One* cut his hair a few times before and thought I might be able to help him out a little that night. I didn't think he'd really take my offer seriously, but to my surprise, he did without any hesitation. He demonstrated the technique first. Then, he took my hand and guided me with a few passes of the clippers over his head. After his hands-on tutorial, he left me to finish the work. When he looked in the mirror at the job I'd done and expressed how pleased he was with the results, he enveloped me with a hug and kiss that said to me I could do no wrong. I remember how he lifted me in that hug, and how my legs wrapped around him as we locked in an embrace. It was yet another time that we'd shared an intimate experience that tightened our love bond. He gave me the honor of cutting his hair that night, and he, on that same trip, championed the reins of doing something for me that, for all of my young adult life, only my dad had done.

We had taken my car to New Orleans because it was time for some standard maintenance—oil change, tire rotation, and just that good "lookin' at". My dad had taught me how to go and have that done so I could manage while I was away from him, but any time I was home, he took my car to get the maintenance it needed. The morning after my first barbering experience, I awoke, and *The One* wasn't in bed with me. He'd gotten up early and taken my car to have it serviced. We'd talked about it on the way to New Orleans, so he knew it was time for an oil change. He knew it was time to have the tires rotated. He knew all the things that my dad would normally check for or have checked because I'd shared that with him. *The One* made sure all of that was done. When he returned, he had that look of accomplishment on his face and an air about him that boasted of having taken care of his woman, knowing she would be pleased. He knew he'd done something that checked a worry off of my list and lightened my load. The protector in him wanted to have me as stress free as possible, and he'd done that so many times in our relationship. That day was different, though, because just like that, the job of caring for my car was no longer solely my daddy's honor. *The One* had staked that claim. Love bond, love bond, love bond, and next steps, and next steps, and...

All of that is what made it easy for us to enter into a place of physical intimacy that night that we'd never experienced together, causing me to almost give myself completely to *The One* and making it more and more difficult for me to set and maintain boundaries. I had already opened Door #1 in Dallas by allowing him to sleep in my hotel room after there was already an understanding that he wouldn't. That door would never be closed again. The events behind Door #1 eventually led to the opening of Door #2, which was my sometimes staying the night at *The One's* apartment, and after that door was opened, there was no closing it. Then, Doors #3 and #4 and on and on and on. Even when I tried to reset boundaries or establish new ones, they didn't last. It was never long before we were right back into our same routines. And so was the cycle. Love bond, then next steps.

Trust, then next steps.

Love bond, then next steps.

Trust, then next steps.

We spent some time traveling back and forth to *The One's* hometown too. Not long after our trip to New Orleans, we attended one of his cousins' basketball games at *The One's* former high school. The game was a really big deal. I recall that it may have even been the championship game because the entire family was there, and *The One* refused to miss it. When we arrived at the game, I got right on in there with his family. I didn't feel like a stranger at all; I felt like I was with my own family. That night, I slept in his sister's old room, and he slept in his old room. We were accustomed to sleeping with each other at that point, so it was weird, but it was also weirdly refreshing. I remember thinking that night that that was how things were supposed to be. I remember feeling a weight of guilt for not setting a better example. I would feel that weight countless more times throughout our relationship, especially in the months following that trip.

The next morning, the entire family had breakfast, and afterward, I had a special moment with just his dad. We talked for quite some time, and I learned that *The One* had never taken anyone home to "seriously" meet his family since he'd been at Tech. I had been the only one. He was scheduled to graduate just a few weeks after that visit. Love bond, love bond, love bond…

After *The One* graduated, he accepted a job about a half an hour away from Tech. The change in the dynamics of our relationship could have certainly broken us because all we had then were weekends, but the "us" that we were didn't see obstacles. We never even had any major talks about how we would maintain our relationship. We just did what we had to do. Not once was there a question that we were still—and would still—be together. Every weekend we were together, either at his new apartment or mine. Sometimes, we'd be so hungry for time with each other that we'd get together during the week too, no matter how unfeasible.

I was in love, and my entanglement in those emotions was clouding my ability to lean completely on the Holy Spirit. When I was with *The One*, I released all inhibitions, and God began to show me that He wanted me to love *Him* like that. He showed me that that type of love is to be reserved for Him first, and until I loved Him like that, I wasn't fit to love anyone else in that way. He showed me that if I *did* love anyone (or anything) that way without loving Him first, it would destroy me. And it actually already had. I was the happiest, most miserable person I knew.

Flip the Script

Summer 2001, I went back to KAA, and I didn't work only one term; I worked the entire summer, from May to July. Camp was the nudge in my spirit that made me look at how I was living life with *The One* versus how I *should be* living it. It was my annual checkup. My detox, so to speak, and that summer detoxed me for sure. When I got back to Louisiana, I didn't break up with *The One* because I knew he might be expecting it. But I wanted to.

Pretty much that whole next school year, I lived with the same push and pull that I'd experienced with *The One* for over a year. I was still in God's Word, spending crazy time in His presence, attending church regularly, and serving as the spiritual advisor of the gospel choir. It was unbelievable to me how the Lord would still give me messages to teach the gospel choir on Wednesday nights. I would still get words of encouragement and guidance for my friends, and I would still receive powerful revelation and understanding for myself, but I felt so unworthy. I was uncomfortable and unsure and afraid. I wanted to hide under a rock because I knew my life wasn't an acceptable reflection of what it means to walk in righteousness, but I still wanted to be with *The One*. I distinctly remember it being the top of the spring quarter that school year, late January 2002, right after the holiday season, when I took a long, hard look at my turmoil and knew I couldn't do it anymore. There was nothing honorable about enforcing rules in my dorm and breaking them myself. There was nothing honorable about "saying" who I was while "being" someone else. God was after my heart, and I was finally ready to surrender.

Over the next few months, I became unbearably uncomfortable with *The One*. I loved him with all of my heart, but suddenly, I didn't want him near me. My spirit grieved every time we were together. My body was with him, but my mind, soul, and emotions had finally gotten on one accord with my spirit and pulled me toward wholehearted devotion to the Lord. I tried to fight the disconnect I was feeling, but I couldn't. I knew if I stayed with him, I'd be more miserable than ever, and I'd had enough of that.

I would try to explain to *The One* how I was feeling, but it always came across as spiritually overboard or my trying to be holier than thou because he just didn't get it. And I could see how it looked to him. I actually wasn't mad at him for not understanding; I knew the things of the Spirit didn't make sense to him. There we were, in the most amazing relationship, both desiring it to end in marriage, and in his eyes, I learned later, would have definitely been the case, but I didn't know how to stand firm in my convictions to honor God. I was weak and couldn't trust myself with *The One*, and I'd known that from the very beginning. I knew I would continue to fall, and because I knew I wanted to please God and grow in Him, I had to leave *The One*. I just had to end it.

The One vs. THE One

The One had been invited to a banquet that was happening at Tech one Friday night that April. He asked me to go with him. Of course, we planned for him to stay with me in my apartment that weekend so he could attend the event and so we could have some time together.

I didn't feel like myself at all that weekend. It was as if I were walking around in a dense personal fog. At the banquet, I physically sat next to *The One*, but I was in another place in my mind. I felt dirty. I hadn't been sweating or anything, but I had a sudden urge to get out of the dress I was in and step into something that was freshly washed. I even squirmed in my seat because of the discomfort. I'd never experienced anything like it before. It was like an out-of-body encounter. I was annoyed by the sound of his voice. And when he put his arm around me, it felt like a ton of weight was resting on my shoulders. I couldn't hold conversation with our friends who shared a table with us that night. I was dazed and very obviously discontent, so I decided to leave early. I just couldn't stay, and I remember very vividly, within myself, being done with "us" right then.

When I got to my apartment, I began to walk the floor and pray. I told God what I was feeling. I cried like a baby and begged

Him to wash me clean. I wasn't oblivious to what was happening. I knew the push and pull I'd been experiencing was coming to an end, and God's pull was winning.

After I changed into some freshly washed bed clothes, I made myself comfortable on the couch and fell asleep there. I wanted *The One* to sleep in the bed without me whenever he got in from the banquet that night. There was no way I would've been able to peacefully sleep beside him. He knew, from the way I'd left the banquet, that something was wrong, and that next day he tried to talk about it. I shrugged all his attempts off with the "I'm okay" and "Nothing's wrong" leave-me-alone-about-it answers because I was still processing what was going on. In times past, when I'd tried to explain myself to him, it didn't work, so I needed the Lord to take the lead, and for once, I stepped back and waited for His direct guidance. The more time I spent with the Lord, in His Word and in prayer, the ickier I felt whenever I even talked to *The One* in the days following the banquet. Every day, I was disconnecting more and more from "us".

One night, maybe about a week or so after the banquet, I finally got my words together enough to at least try to explain what was happening with me. I'd spoken with *The One* earlier that day and let him know we needed to talk. When he called, I remember saying very few words before I began crying my eyes out. I had been battling in my spirit all that day. *The One* was trying so hard to understand the root of my tears. I attempted to gather myself to stop crying long enough to explain, but the tears wouldn't stop. I was trying to explain to him how I felt about being the person I was when I was with him. I was telling him I didn't want to be that person anymore. I explained that I wanted to be who I was when I was learning the things of God with people who believed like I believed and lived how I wanted to live. I remember becoming so weak that I didn't even have the strength to continue standing. My knees buckled eventually, and I went from standing to kneeling, and from kneeling to lying on the floor. I rocked back and forth on my side, praying and wailing. I removed the phone from my ear and stretched my arm out with the phone still in my hand. I screamed out to God and the phone dropped. I don't know if *The One* was still on the other end or not, but as I was praying, I began to hear myself pray in an unknown language as the Holy Spirit gave utterance. It alarmed me at first, but I didn't stop. I let it flow because I knew my spirit was crying out. I don't know how long I prayed in the Spirit before I came to, but I knew when I got up off of that floor, we were done. I felt like I was standing at a crossroads. I could see the *Dead End* sign before me. I could go left into a life with Christ and give up my idol of *The One* and learn how to love God that way, or I could go with *The One* and continue to live without the peace that I so desperately desired.

Our conversations after that were few and far between, and the ones that we did have were forced and strained. We no longer had anything to talk about, and he saw me slowly slipping away from "us". It was like night and day. *The One* wanted to get things right, but at that point, there was nothing else he could do. The Lord had my heart. Instantly, my tolerance for anything that displeased the Lord was low. My spiritual senses were heightened. The work was done in me.

I went on to KAA summer 2002, from May to July again, and I broke up with *The One* for good while I was at camp. I didn't want to go back to Louisiana still carrying our dead relationship. I meant business, and I wanted it done. I wanted Jesus, and that was it. But of course we had too much history for there to be an immediate and clean cut.

I changed my phone number and my email address. I had to let mutual friends of ours know that I couldn't have contact with *The One*. I needed to clear my space so I could purge. Naturally, he was devastated, but it had to be done. We would've ended up right back where we left off because where we left off and what we had was all we knew. He wasn't ready to grow in Christ with me, which could've made a difference because we could've grown together, but I was ready to give the Lord all of me. He wasn't. We would always have differences if we didn't agree on that. And it hurt. My heart hurt so badly that at times I experienced physical pain from the anguish. I begged God to let me have him. I cried and begged and begged and cried. But nope. The Lord wasn't havin' it. I had a call on my life that could not be fulfilled if I was going to be idolizing *The One*. I had to release him.

As much as it hurt…and LORD, did it hurt…I knew, even through the pain…

He wasn't it either.

Out in the Open with
The One

It may have been hurtful to have gone through it, but it would be quite the misfortune to have learned nothing in the process.

There are things the Lord showed me from my time with *The One* that helped shape me into the woman I am today. I want to lay some of those things out in the open for you.

Out in the Open with The One #1 – He can be a good man, but if he's not a God man, you lose.

I mentioned being unequally yoked in the previous chapter, but I need to revisit it here. The term "yoked" is used in farming. When animals (oxen mostly) are placed side by side to work farm land, they are yoked together, or bound together, by the neck with a yoke (usually a wooden board) so the work can be done more efficiently. Having two animals doing the job versus having only one just makes sense. Farmers would usually put oxen together that could work with the same intensity. If there was one that was strong and one that was weak, the strong one would do most of the work and simply pull the other along, dragging its dead weight. The weaker ox's only concern, then, would be survival. Effectiveness and attention to the task would be gone.

Now liken this to my relationship with *The One*, or your relationship with someone of unequal yoking. I was getting instructions from the Lord; I understood my purpose. I was studying God's Word and He was showing me what to do to make disciples on my campus. I was on the path, doing all I knew to do to reach lost souls, but I was connected to someone who wasn't. My vision for the assignment was clear, and I was working to see it come to pass, but not the one who was yoked up with me. He didn't see the plan. He didn't even desire to make disciples, so his drive didn't equal mine. I was running full speed ahead, excited about where I was going, but I was dragging the dead spiritual weight of the one who was connected to me. He wasn't excited about where we were going because he wasn't even moving in that direction. How unfortunate to be yoked with someone who's supposed to be the leader and supposed to have the vision for "the job," but they can't see! How unfortunate to be yoked with someone who's supposed to be the leader and supposed to have the vision for "the job," but they're too weak to pull the load because they're not feeding on the nutrients (the Word of God) necessary for the work! How unfortunate it is!

There are far too many of us who are much too comfortable with accepting a man because he's a "good" man. Just because he has a "good" job making "good" money with "good" benefits and he's "good" to you doesn't mean he's "good" *for* you. *The One* was a good man, you hear me? He would break his neck to make sure I was taken care of. He could cook and clean. He was very thoughtful. He would see a need of mine and just meet it without my asking. He kept my car clean. He *wanted* to talk to me, intimately and regularly, and he initiated most of our conversation. He would shout from the rooftops to any and every one that he loved me and wanted only me. BUT…he wasn't ready to live for God. That made all of the "good" stuff null and void.

He can be a "good" man, but if he's not a God man, you lose. You see, you live in a body and you possess a soul, but you are a spirit being, and your spirit *has to be* satisfied. Your spirit *has to* agree with the spirit of the one to whom you're yoked. If the spirit you're connected to is in opposition with yours, you will be miserable. It doesn't mean he's not a good person. Nope. Sure doesn't. It *does* mean, though, that you're not good for each other. He's not God's best for you if he can't lead your spirit, and you're not God's best for him if you can't follow his. And that's that. A woman who is submitted to the Lord and is walking in purpose should never settle for a "good" man. She must be led by a God man.

Out in the Open with The One #2 – You have to set boundaries to avoid sexual temptation and live by them.

It was ridiculous of me to tell *The One* we weren't going to have sex and then turn around and allow him in bed with me. I was adding logs to a fire that I was foolishly wishing wouldn't burn. And how dare I get mad if the fire *did* burn and he wanted from me what I thought I shouldn't have to give! It was so unfair to him. I was stirring things up and making a mess that was pretty much forced upon him. I set up a situation of which he unknowingly became a victim. Had I honored the boundaries I'd set, I could've kept us from headache and heartache.

I had no real boundaries with *The One* because we weren't working *together* to uphold any. If we were both as serious about living for the Lord, we would have *wanted* to honor each other and wouldn't have allowed each other to compromise the boundaries we'd set. We needed to hold each other accountable. That was a part of the problem (unequally yoked).

This—lack of boundaries with *The One*—was strikingly similar to the lack of boundaries I had with *Puppy Love*. In high school, our parents, of course, weren't letting us spend nights with each other, but they were pretty hands off. Had not I, within myself, had the strict adherence to no sex, it could easily have been a part of our relationship. I wasn't mindful and intentional about keeping myself "out of the fire," and that's where a lot of us miss it. Right there. We have no intentional plan in place to keep us from "being burned".

I wouldn't dare tell you that you need to set boundaries and not leave you with some practical ones to implement when you enter into a dating/courting relationship. These are things I wish I would've introduced and/or held firm to with *The One*.

1. Have a curfew. This means you're out of each other's places by a certain time that's reasonably set by both of you. If you decide to attend an event that goes on past the

curfew that you two set, make it your business to head straight home once the event is over. Get into the practice, and soon it'll be like second nature.

2. Go on group dates with at least one other couple, and do this most of your time together. Group dating doesn't mean you're connected at the hip with the other couple when you're out, but you decide to arrive together, remain in each other's general vicinity, and leave together. For example, you all could go to an amusement park one day and have completely separate agendas while there and just decide to meet up in a designated spot at the appointed time.

3. When you decide to go on dates alone, go *out*. Determine together when and where the dates alone will be, but definitely go out. Don't stay in.

4. My personal conviction is to not kiss. I'll talk more about this with *The Secret* later in the book. It leads to other things, and it awakens love before its time.

5. If you're going to hang out in each other's homes, plan out the evening. Know exactly what you're going to do. You don't have to be as rigid as having an actual printed program in place for the evening, but know that you have something in place for the time you plan to be together. After everything you plan to do is done, it's time for each of you to be in your own homes.

6. End conversations and textersations before they become late-night marathons. Allow each other adequate rest; you have to care for one another. And we know what kinds of conversations tend to get stirred up in the late night hours anyway.

7. Each of you needs an accountability partner. You need a female accountability partner, and he needs a male accountability partner. This is someone with whom you will be brutally honest about what's happening in the relationship and about what's happening with you so they can pray with and for you, give you godly counsel, and encourage you to honor God in the relationship.

8. An accountability couple is a good addition or alternative to personal accountability partners. If you decide to seek out an accountability couple, that couple should be a married couple that is interested in seeing you honor God in your relationship and can give you wise, godly counsel.

It's possible to date and honor one another with boundaries. I've seen it. I've done it. I've also seen this: **Every time you break one of your own boundaries, you break down a wall of your credibility.** You become known for letting down your guard, and he then *expects* you to do so. He expects to be able to break you down, and this could cause him to lose respect for you since you don't do what you say you're going to do. And believe it or not, it can break down the trust in other areas.

Out in the Open with The One #3 – A man who loves and honors you will only do what you allow. If you don't allow it, he won't do it.

- I said, "No sex." He said, "Okay."
- If I would've said we weren't going to spend time in each other's bedrooms, he would've been fine with it.
- If I would've never let *The One* spend the night with me, he never would have.

In the beginning of our relationship, I'd set a standard, and because he wanted to be with me, he met that standard. He would've been fine with whatever parameters I set because he loved and respected me. It's when I began to bend those standards and compromise my own limits that the relationship hit its demise. And even then, *The One* was only doing what I allowed.

So, know this: Woman, you hold the key. If you set the bar, he'll either reject it, or he'll step up. If he upholds the standard, great. If he rejects it, that's great too because that lets you know he's not worth your time. He will only do to you and with you what you allow.

Out in the Open with The One #4 – Give a relationship marriage privileges, and you'll behave like you're in a marriage. Then when it's over, it'll hurt like a divorce.

Why do you think divorce is so ugly? Why do you think God hates divorce? It hurts all who are involved because the oneness that was formed in marriage—the two families that became one, the two homes that became one in some cases, the two bodies that became one, the two lifestyles that became one—are no more. Relationships that carry on like marriage hurt the same way. There's a ripping. A tearing. A dividing. And the rift, although over time repaired and healed, always leaves a scar.

Out in the Open with The One #5 – The longer you stay, the harder it is to leave. The "Love Bond" is real!

Don't you dare be afraid to cut ties when you know the relationship shouldn't go on any more. The longer you stay, the more connections you'll form in different facets of the relationship. And the more connections you have, the harder the chain will be to break.

Yes, I changed my number and my email address when *The One* and I broke up, but I only had to take such drastic measures because of how strong our "Love Bond" was. This doesn't have to be the case for you. Had I ended the relationship sooner, that probably wouldn't have had to be the case for me either.

You have to know that there's life after *him*, whoever he is, and you have to know that God's got you. I wasn't playing around with the Lord when I told Him I wanted to wholeheartedly "delight myself in Him."[14] And I promise you, just as the rest of that scripture says, as a result of my delighting in Him, He has given me the desires of my heart. I couldn't tiptoe around *The One* forever and play around with lust. I couldn't continue to break the heart of the God who created me and wanted to fulfill His work on earth through me. And you can't either.

If that relationship you're in is not it, and you know it (because we always do), do yourself that favor and leave sooner than later. You know when your spirit is not free, and you know when your spirit is not satisfied with who it's connected to. Don't make it any harder than it has to be. Determine that now is the best time to leave.

Out in the Open with The One #6 – Abstain from the very appearance of evil.[9]

Don't be a stumbling block in someone's path.[15]

There's no telling how many people were misled by some of the things I was doing while I was with *The One*. I was a poor example of what it looks like to live as a Christian, and an even poorer example of Christlike leadership. When I was an RA, my residents saw *The One* in my dorm staying past curfew. And what does that say to onlookers? What does that look like to someone who may have been watching me for a Godly example to follow?

---

[14] Psalm 37:4, *Holy Bible*
[15] I Corinthians 8:9, *Holy Bible*

Later, when I was a hall director, other residents saw *The One* in my dorm apartment, sleeping there when he shouldn't have been. Even worse, I had a member of my staff who knew I was spending some nights away from the dorm because I was putting her in charge. Reprehensible!

Like it or not, there are people watching you to know what it means to live a life that pleases God and reflects Jesus Christ. We're always an example to those who are watching and to those who are under our care; God's Word reminds us of this. You're responsible for being His example in the earth. When we mess up and knowingly continue to walk in sin, we make others think it's acceptable and it has the potential to lead them astray. This is what it means to be a stumbling block in someone's "path to Jesus". You don't want that blood on your hands.

Tweet your takeaways from *The One*.
#HWIETheOne

If it resonated with you,
it can probably help someone else.

Tag me in your posts on Twitter and Instagram.

Let's connect!

@ianthasinsight

Rebound

The numbness will make you go with the flow even though your heart is screaming for you to swim upstream.

It was Fall 2022, and it was over with *The One*. I wasn't even thinking about being in another relationship, and it was clear that my family, for reasons different than my own, wasn't thinking about my moving on either. It had been a few months after the breakup when I learned that my mom and *The One* had been engaging in occasional conversations by phone. Neither of them had fully accepted that things were over. *They* still had to break up. Needless to say, their connection, no matter how innocent or well-intended, was making it difficult for me to move forward. I found myself explaining to my mom, more than once, and the rest of my family too, that they needed to completely cut ties with *The One* for my well-being. It was just too hard for me to still "have him around." *(Years later, when my mom and I talked about that time in my life, it was so refreshing. By then, she had gotten saved and was growing in her Christian faith, so she finally really understood my reason for the breakup. She let me know that she was proud of what I'd done for the sake of peace in my own heart and for my growth in Christ.)*

I needed to purge and disconnect myself, as much as possible, from *The One*, but because of our mutual friends, campus connections, and family ties, it didn't come without considerable challenges. I didn't let the challenges stop me, though. I was resolute in my decision to give myself completely to the Lord and separate myself from anyone and anything I realized I idolized. And what better way to do that than by creating new memories with someone else? Although those weren't my thoughts then, I can look back now and see that that's exactly what was happening. I never actually said to myself, *Okay, the best way to move forward from* The One *is to be with another one.* My common sense wouldn't even allow me to utter such foolishness, but I subconsciously, and somewhat automatically, did just that. I made the mistake that so many women make after a relationship ends—I walked too quickly into another one. As I said before, I wasn't exactly looking to be with anyone, but for reasons I still can't confidently explain, I didn't reject the next guy who sought my attention just a few short months after all was said and done with *The One*. Lord knows I should have turned a blind eye to him, though, because rebound relationships are almost always a mistake.

Rewind to Rebound

I met *Rebound* my second summer at KAA in 2001 when *The One* and I were still together. He was among the host of people who served on the KAA staff that I gained lasting friendships with throughout my four-year stint. We were all on fire for God and excited about spreading His truth. Every summer, the camp staff, which was comprised of college students and young adults, would live together, work together, laugh and cry together, and pray and teach children the Word of God together. We grew to love each other like family. Shoot, we *were* (and are) family. And just because camp was in session only in the summer didn't mean we didn't keep in touch throughout the school year. In fact, some of my most memorable road trips are the trips I took with camp friends, visiting other camp friends, or traveling and meeting up with camp friends just to hang out. It's how we stayed connected.

Rebound was my brother in Christ. I didn't even find him physically attractive, so it was hard for me to see him as anything other than family. I did, however, adore his love for the Lord and was intrigued by his ability to share the Word of God with an unfeigned ease and passionate conviction all in one whip. I watched him from afar, but I saw his "God life" as if I were up close. Turns out he saw me too, and that's how we connected. We connected over our love for sharing God's Word.

I remember emails we'd write during the school year about how God was using us on our college campuses to teach His Word. I was always encouraged by those emails. *Rebound* was a gleam of hope for me, a very present reminder that there were men out there who weren't ashamed to walk boldly in Christ and serve Him with their whole heart. That's what made him stand out in my mind. Nothing else. Until, of course, he expressed a desire to be more than a brother.

When I was still with *The One*, *Rebound* was aware of the relationship. He never made any advances or interacted with me as anything other than a friend during that time. As I said, our communication throughout the school year was via email every now and then to encourage each other or to share what we were experiencing. Our communication while serving at camp was minimal because men and boys were housed on one side of the camp, and women and girls on the other side, joining together only for meals, morning camp-wide events, and evening programs and parties. Even then, we were constantly on duty, guiding and/or instructing the children who were in our care. Co-ed interaction, was limited, so whatever feelings *Rebound* developed for me were as a result of those interactions—conversations every now and then at camp, and occasional emails throughout the school year.

Or could it have been that one time?

Stranded

No one, and I mean *no one* had more air travel drama than I had in my college travel days. LORD! My flights were always delayed. I seemed to always be on flights that had to make emergency landings, and it was not uncommon for my luggage to be lost in transit. It was just the story of my travel life.

Since I'd grown somewhat accustomed to the ups and downs with my excursions and was learning to just go with the flow, when the flight was delayed for this particular trip from Colorado, I wasn't surprised. I wasn't upset or nervous until I realized that that flight's delay would prevent me from making my connection flight in Houston that would get me back to Monroe, Louisiana. I knew that by the time I would have made it to the connection flight, it would have already departed. And that's exactly what happened. I was stuck in Texas for the night. I would have to take the first flight out the following morning. I would also have to wait until that next morning to be reunited with my luggage; it was already on its way to Louisiana without me.

My brain instantly kicked into high gear. I had to figure out what to do that night because sleeping at the airport was not an Iantha option. I was just about to search out hotels near the airport when I remembered that I knew a few camp people in Houston who I could call. I knew seeing a familiar face had the potential to make my predicament a little less dreadful. I called my now best friend, who I met my second year at KAA, to get a phone number for someone we knew, and in that conversation, she said, "You know *Rebound* is in Houston too."

I said, "He sure is."

After making a call here and a call there, it wasn't long before we ended up with *Rebound's* number.

I called.

He answered.

I explained my situation, and he immediately responded with, "Which airport?"

After unveiling the details and making sure he'd be able to get me to the airport early that next morning, I said, "Please come and get me."

I was tired and a bit frustrated. I had my carry-on bag that held my toiletries and the "if I'm ever stranded" necessities, and that provided some comfort for me in the moment, but I was also unshakably cognizant of the fact that I had no luggage. *The One* was on my mind and in my ear on my cell phone because he was completely frazzled back in Louisiana. My not getting back to the expected destination at the scheduled time, although I was very clearly safe and sound, just didn't sit well with him. He thought the worst. Poor thing. He was concerned for my safety and was no doubt feeling out of control in that moment because he couldn't be there to protect me. And then, to completely tip the scale, I told him that I would be staying at my friend's place, my *male* friend from KAA, the place he loathed because he believed every summer, little by little, it took me away from him.

Although I would literally only be in Houston long enough for a light snooze before having to get back to the airport, *The One* wasn't feelin' it. I couldn't dwell on it, though. I already had enough turmoil with my situation; I didn't need him adding to it. I'd settled within myself that I would deal with his concerns once I got back to Louisiana.

Rebound was a good host for the few hours I was with him. He offered his bed for my slumber and said he'd take the couch, and although a chivalrous gesture, I was completely uncomfortable with even the thought of sleeping in his bed. I told him the couch was fine with me because I didn't need to fall into a deep sleep anyway; I would need to be up and ready to roll in a few hours. I wasn't comfortable showering in his apartment either, so I did the absolute bare minimum to prepare for my light nap and so I'd be decent enough to travel the next morning, and I peacefully rested in the safety of *Rebound's* couch.

I woke in a few hours with great anticipation to board a plane to Monroe. After a quick dash in the bathroom to freshen up, I walked out to find *Rebound* waiting at the front door of his apartment, ready to escort me to the parking lot where my chariot awaited. Once in his truck, we took the short ride to the airport, making it there in perfect time. *Rebound* walked me in to make sure everything was okay and that my flight would definitely be leaving as scheduled. When he saw that all was well, he went on.

Maybe that did it. Maybe when *Rebound* had to come to my rescue and protect me, he realized he wanted to be more than just friends. My feelings, however, certainly hadn't changed. I was just grateful to have had someone get me from the airport to relieve my stress and get me back to the airport the next morning so I could get back to school. I would've done the same for him or any other of my brothers or sisters had they been in such dire straits.

Too Close for Comfort

If that wasn't when his thoughts about me took a shift, it had to have been later that same school year when *Rebound's* basketball team played at Tech, and I was somehow chosen to sing the national anthem at that game. I *still* don't know how that happened, but my guess is that it had something to do with having been a member of the gospel choir. I knew his school was coming to play ours; he'd called to let me know, and although I hardly went to any games, I stayed for that one to see *Rebound* play. *The One* was with me.

I had to be on the floor before the game to do a sound check and get technical directions. Just as I was finishing up the sound check, *Rebound's* team ran out to warm up. He spotted me and waved. I waved back. After warm-ups were done and it was time for me to sing, I walked out and stood at half court with a perfect view of the players as they stood to salute the flag. *Rebound* smiled at me as I sang. The whole song. Literally. From "O! Say can you see…" to "…and the home of the brave."

Mental note.

After the game, *The One* and I waited on the floor for the team to leave the locker room so I could introduce him to *Rebound*. They shook hands and had man-to-man small talk. Then, *Rebound* walked over and hugged me. We exchanged a few words, and he put a card in my hand—a card that had nothing but a lengthy hand-written message to me on the inside.

Mental note.

Again.

Iantha Ussin

I held the card in my hand as *The One* and I walked from the gym floor to the upper level of the coliseum and from the coliseum for what seemed like an eternity to the parking lot. I didn't dare put it in my purse for fear of it looking like I was trying to keep something from him.

It was an uncomfortable ride back to my apartment that night as I silently read the card for the first time in the passenger seat. I thought it would say something like, "Thanks for comin' holla at ya boy at the game," or "I appreciate your support," which was the way we always communicated. But it was evident from my first glance at the lengthiness of the note that it was about to stir up friction between *The One* and me. *The One* was already weirded out about my having stayed at *Rebound's* place when I was stuck in Houston, and we'd finally gotten past that. Then, like a pesky, relentless hangnail, out of nowhere came the card.

It was mind-blowing to me that *Rebound* had carefully prepared his thoughts in advance and placed them in a card that he knew he'd give to me at that game. After reading his message a million times over the next few days, I could see that his thoughts toward me were not at all what they had been at camp only about five or six months prior. I don't remember the message verbatim, but I know he praised me for being a woman of God and for having a standard for other Christian women to follow. He said he was grateful for our friendship and glad we had the opportunity to meet. There were some other sentiments in the message, but the general tone of the card was enough for me to see that *Rebound* had an affection for me, clearly beyond friendship, that I couldn't reciprocate.

That night, *Rebound's* card and his interaction with me did nothing but reopen what I thought was a sutured wound. *The One* had always tried really hard to be understanding of the brother-sister relationship I had with *Rebound;* I had to give him that. It was because he knew me and trusted me and knew I wouldn't do

99

anything to hurt him. But he didn't know *Rebound* and he certainly didn't trust him. We never had to address anything with any other guy throughout our time together. It was *that* relationship, a relationship that had already made moves beyond *The One's* control, that bothered him. It was the one that he could never really figure out, the thorn in his side. *The One* always felt, somewhere in the back of his mind, that *Rebound's* intentions were never just brotherly. He'd said a few times before, "Just like you know women, and you know when them girls ain't no good, I know dudes, and he don't wanna just be your friend."

I knew how he felt. I knew it bothered him to have the guy who'd rescued his girl "move into" her personal space, but he didn't argue with me, and he didn't even really talk about it. He *did* let me see that he wasn't happy, and he *did* let me know, one more time, that *Rebound's* intentions were for more than just friendship. And for the first time, I could see it too. That meant I had to make some moves. I didn't want *The One* to think I was encouraging *Rebound's* affection toward me because I definitely wasn't. I was shocked to see that *Rebound* had flipped the switch like that, and the more I thought about it, the more it perturbed me. I didn't want unnecessary friction in my relationship, so I cut communication with *Rebound*. I didn't email him anymore. And I think *Rebound* knew the deal too because he didn't email me either. And he didn't call.

Time went on, and *The One* and I moved past it. *The One* could see that I didn't want *Rebound*, after I convinced him over and over again. Nonetheless, that was probably what did it. That had to be when *Rebound* decided he would have me as more than just a sister and friend, even if he had to be quiet for a while before he could.

Iantha Ussin

The Pounce

May 2022, when the school year ended, I went back to KAA for the entire summer, and it was the summer I broke it off with *The One* for good. It was also the summer that *Rebound* made a short visit to camp, which was a KAA tradition for those, like *Rebound*, who no longer served on staff. From the moment he stepped foot on the campgrounds, making it his business to have our eyes meet in the midst of my busyness with my campers, it was clear that a conversation was in our near future. We hadn't spoken since that card, and it was time to connect all the dots that stood still in the sphere of space and time that kept us at bay. The magnetic pull between us was hard to miss, and there was no sense in fighting it.

I was on the clock, of course, but he wasn't, so that meant whenever I had a free moment in my schedule, he was readily available. We talked a lot the few days he was there, and of course, somewhere in those conversations, we talked about *The One* and me and that we weren't together anymore. Our chats after that day started off light and familiar, but it wasn't long before *Rebound* swooped in, his every word wrapped in a tone that was reminiscent of what I'd read in his card. He wanted more. And it seemed, now that he was free to say what he wanted, he always had.

Things were becoming blurrily clear at that point. I could see what was going on every time we talked, as his eyes studied my face with a new, unfamiliar intentness, but it still didn't seem real. This wasn't how he interacted with me. Maybe some other girl, but not *me*.

I could hear his voice as I always had, but there was something new to his sound. There was a mellow gentleness that, without a doubt, was conjured up just for me. I was dumbfounded, yet curious. Nervous, but still sure. Wanting to pump the brakes, but continuing to lie back for the ride. Heart screaming for me to turn around and pedal uphill, but the rest of me too numb to move.

I wasn't ready, and I knew I wasn't, but I didn't even know how to stop what was happening. It was as if I'd taken a debilitating drug that incapacitated every limb and bridled my tongue, leaving only my eyes with their normal functionality. So, helplessly, I watched it all unfold. I don't remember when it happened, and I don't remember how, but somewhere between those talks at camp in July and my journey back to Louisiana Tech in August, we'd become "a thing". I'd fallen into the trap.

Numb

It was my last quarter at Tech. I remember talking to *Rebound* every day that quarter, and every word of our conversations— every day—felt forced. I would find myself cringing sometimes at the sight of his name when my phone rang with his calls because very early on, I realized we were talking only about the things of God. That's all we'd ever discussed as friends, so that's all we knew. Talking about anything outside of that—school, life in general, my interests, his interests—just took too much work. It wasn't natural. The magnetic pull that had ushered us into the inevitable, long-awaited talk that day at camp was no more. In fact, that day would be the last time I ever detected any organic magnetism between us. It was painfully obvious thereafter, to me at least, that we had absolutely no chemistry.

Just because *Rebound* loved God, I reasoned that being with him was much better than being in a relationship with someone who wasn't ready to walk with God and who couldn't understand me spiritually. I was so busy trying to grab hold of the "God factor" that had been missing with *The One* that I closed my eyes to seeing that all *Rebound* had (for me) *was* the "God factor". I was forcing myself to see him as physically attractive too. He was not an unattractive man, by far, and that I clearly acknowledged, but he wasn't my kind of attractive. He didn't—like I would say to my friends about men sometimes—turn my head away from what I was doing. And I knew I wasn't his kind of attractive either. I knew it from the way he looked and didn't look at me whenever he would look at me, or not look at me for looking at someone else. And within me, there was always this knowing that he didn't care for me the way *The One* had. He liked me, but he didn't care for me deeply. He *couldn't* because he didn't know *me*. We had nothing.

Still, I made efforts to recreate the same closeness between us that was naturally existent between *The One* and me. I did things like put up pictures around my apartment of him and of us as a couple as I'd done with *The One* and me before, but it was just too much too soon. I didn't even know *Rebound* like that. I hadn't created any our-pictures-deserve-to-be-up-around-my-apartment memories with him like I had with *The One*. There was no way he could have "that place" with me in less than a month that *The One* had earned over much more meaningful time. But I couldn't see that. I couldn't see that all I really wanted was to just still be in love, and I couldn't see that I was hurting because I wasn't. I couldn't see that I was literally having withdrawals from not having someone to genuinely connect with, and I couldn't see that I was hurting because I didn't. I couldn't see that those withdrawals had formed a void within me, and I couldn't see that I was just trying to fill it. I was trying, in every way, to reach back and grab anything that felt familiar so that hurt wouldn't be there. So the void wouldn't be there. So maybe even I wouldn't be there feeling what I was feeling. But I was there. And the void was there. And the hurt was there. And *Rebound* was there, talking marriage.

Yes, you read that right. He began talking marriage.

I was flattered that *Rebound* would already know I could be his wife, but it completely perplexed me at the same time. I was fully aware that I hadn't earned a place with him that warranted our becoming one, and I couldn't understand, for the life of me, how he didn't know that too. I often found myself in the Twilight Zone as we talked, simply answering questions as he asked, but never fully engaging. Hesitation was seemingly nonexistent in him, though, and because *he* seemed to be so sure, I eventually betrayed my caution and the unsettling within me and took on the idea of marriage as my own, going with the flow, even though it was ridiculously uncomfortable for me. I began to rationalize that maybe we just needed more time together for things to click for us. I figured it would only be a matter of time before the awkwardness would subside, but I couldn't have been more wrong. Nothing could have prepared me for just how awkward our little make-believe love bubble had yet to become.

Too Much!

One weekend that September, after only a little over a month into "our thing," I took a road trip to *Rebound's* school with my sorority sisters who wanted to go there for a football game. It was an opportune time, I thought, to visit *Rebound* on his campus. It was one of my desperate attempts to foster even a glint of genuine romantic chemistry between us. While riding in the car with my sisters, well into the trip and clearly beyond the point of no return, I wanted to bail.

What was I doing? What was I thinking?

Although I'd made plans with him for that weekend and he was expecting me, the whole idea was another Twilight Zone experience. It seemed like a good move when we'd discussed it weeks prior, but with every mile that took us farther away from Louisiana Tech, I regretted having gone through with it more and more. Just like everything else I'd been yessing, I yessed that trip too, hushing all of those screams from my heart's conscience and forging on.

Iantha Ussin

To say it was quite a weekend is an understatement. I didn't even know what to think or how to feel as things began to unfold. Within an hour of my arrival, *Rebound* beckoned me along and began a whirlwind of visits on his campus and around the city, introducing me to every key person of importance in his college life. He was parading me around as his girl, and although, in theory, we were "a thing," I didn't think we were as much of "a thing" as he let on. How in the world was I already meeting all of these people and being invited into their homes to sit with him as his *very serious* significant other, the one he planned to wed? And everyone he introduced me to already knew of his plan to officially ask for my hand in marriage. He'd told them everything! They all had questions about my feelings toward *Rebound* and my hopes for our married life. I was so uncomfortable. It was too much! It was a pressure I wasn't sure of, but at the same time didn't want to combat and make him think my affection didn't match his. I had to stay in it. I'd feel what he felt eventually. That's just how my mind continued to reason. No matter the disconnect, I was still a bit flattered that I'd be introduced to his mentor and other people he respected in the Christian community because wasn't our display that day how Christian couples did things? And wasn't that what I wanted, the godly man who loved the Lord and His Word and was ready to walk wholeheartedly and unashamedly with Him?

Between the visits with all of those people, *Rebound* and I did some riding around the city. While in the car, he explained to me that he wanted us to wear promise rings until he was able to put an engagement ring on my finger. Yet again, I thoughtlessly went along with it. I figured it was just talk for that moment, but then he pulled up to the Christian bookstore and insisted that I go in with him.

Rebound walked me right to some scripture-inscribed, unisex purity rings that he'd obviously scoped out before then and showed me the exact ones we would wear. I was in a daze as he asked me to try on different sizes to see which one fit. Both rings, his and mine, had the same scripture inscribed on them that I unfortunately don't remember. He explained why that scripture was so important and why it mattered so much to him to make a promise like that and seal it with a ring. I couldn't believe what I was hearing! Even more than that, I couldn't believe I was so passive and going along with whatever he said. It was too much!

And in reflecting on that part of the relationship to include it in this book, I couldn't help but think of all of the women who "grin and bear it" in relationships that they know aren't fruitful. She "grins and bears it" because it looks right to the onlookers, or because her parents or other family members think the relationship is right, or because he gives her gifts and money, or because, like me, he wants the relationship and he's so into her that she just goes along with it even though she doesn't feel the same. But because she's not true to herself, she's dying on the inside. In thinking about those women, I began to pray.

God had me to pray specifically for pastors' wives who fit into the "grin and bear it" category. Not female pastors who lead their husbands or lead churches—that's different, and that's a whole different book. He had me to pray for male pastors' wives who serve diligently, helping their husbands with shepherding God's people. God has given me a heart for them. Those who "grin and bear it" have a quiet struggle that only discerning eyes can see. That's another book too.

If only you could have seen me in that store with those quiet clouds of blank thoughts above my head when we were looking at what he was calling promise rings. And if you could've seen my face later that day in the mall when he yanked me off into a jewelry store, chaperoning me from one glass case to another, insisting that I not only look at *wedding* rings, but also try some on so he could "get an idea of what I wanted" for when he would officially propose some time down the line. I thought, *What? Are you even serious right now?*

I couldn't even muster up any excitement; I was floored. There was a part of me that felt sorry for him because I couldn't understand how he couldn't see he was moving way too fast. I was taken aback for a minute while perched on the stool that the jeweler had so graciously pulled out for me before retreating to the other side of the counter. He was eagerly anticipating my requests to try on what he probably thought would be an array of rings. But there was no major try-on-a-thon that day. I had been going along with everything up until that point, but right then was when I finally had to pump the brakes. My awareness of the weightiness of the sanctity of marriage wouldn't let me dive into that moment.

I tried on one ring, deep in a brain fog, still stupefied that we were even in the jewelry store. After that, though, when I came to, I spoke up and told *Rebound* that I was good with having tried on just that one. He tried to talk me into seeing more, but I just couldn't. I knew if he were to really ask me to marry him, I wouldn't be able to peacefully say yes, so I decided to not cheapen the gravity of a moment and decision like that with haphazardness.

Everything after the jewelry store was a blur. I vaguely remember the things we did the remainder of that weekend. Too stunned, and with too little access to the privacy of my own thoughts to process everything that had transpired, I may as well have been comatose. Physically, I was present. Mentally, on another planet.

Fake It 'Til Ya Make It

After that weekend, with the Christian bookstore promise ring residing on my finger, I went back to Tech more confused than before, yet somehow even more committed to the confusion than I'd been since the start of the school year. I began sharing with my friends that *Rebound* and I were talking marriage. I may not have been fully committed in heart, but as a result of months of passive acceptance and matter-of-fact-ness, there was no way I could back out. I had already allowed too much and questioned nothing, so in true Iantha fashion—the new Iantha who clearly didn't even know who she was—I kept rolling with the flow, completely disregarding my own feelings, thoughts, and concerns. As far as *Rebound* knew, I was all in with him, thinking and feeling the exact things he was. And to keep it that way, maybe with a tinge of hope that I'd convince myself to really be all in, I became a walking billboard for "us". I painted our relationship in the most perfect light. The details of what was happening with us were all true, but they were highly romanticized. It was my goal, when talking to my friends about my relationship with *Rebound*, to prove, mostly to myself, that I'd struck gold.

I told them that he'd pursued me, because he had. But I wouldn't dare tell them that his pursuit of me was as unnerving as it was. I told them how he loved the Lord and masterfully taught His Word, but I didn't tell them that all we ever talked about was God because there was absolutely nothing else existent between us. I even talked about how proud he was to show me off at his school that weekend, but they would never know that I could've very well done without that weekend and been just fine. Our relationship wasn't at all what I was fancying it up to be, and I knew it probably never would be.

After I graduated from Tech in November that year, I went on to do a post-graduate semester of study at Focus on the Family Institute (now Focus Leadership Institute) in Colorado Springs. As I began to build relationships with my three roommates and other classmates from all over the United States, our lives became our conversations. The "who are you" and "where did you go to school" and "are you dating anyone" questions were general topics of discussion. I told them about *Rebound*, and again, as I'd done when talking to my friends back at Tech, I built us up. I told my new classmates that *Rebound* and I were planning to get married, and I unveiled the storybook narrative of how that promise ring landed itself on my finger. I gushed about how we'd met at KAA and how he'd rescued me at the airport. I was sure to divulge how he always encouraged me in the Word of God and how our conversations were always centered around the Word. That, I knew, was what my new Christian friends wanted to hear, so I poured it on thick when prompted. I let them know, especially my female classmates, that relationships built in Christ were not only possible, but they were fulfilling. And with every word, I was still trying to convince myself that what I was saying about me could actually be true *for* me.

Rebound was still in school, miles and states away, set to graduate in May. We talked while I was in Colorado, but not much. By that time, I had begun to wrap my mind around the "us" that he'd seen all along. Things were still a little strange for me simply because they'd been that way from the beginning, but they weren't as strange as before. Maybe all the billboarding I'd been doing had finally taken shape within me. Maybe things were beginning to click, I thought, but then I saw how he wasn't making any real effort to make our relationship anything more than phone conversation.

The Truth Revealed

From my relationship with *The One*, I'd learned what it looks like when a man really wants to be with a woman. I had no doubt that if I had still been with *The One*, he would've made at least one trip to Colorado that semester to be with me. He would've wanted to know about my classes and meet my classmates and take in all I was doing. Anything that was of interest to me became important to him, and vice versa, even if we couldn't fully relate to each other's interests. For *The One*, there would've been no excuse. *Rebound*, however, had every excuse. Yes, it was his last semester, and I knew that preparation for graduation could be a doozy, but I just knew, regardless of what was happening in his life, if he wanted to be there to share what was happening in my life, he would've made a way, especially if I was who he was planning to marry.

That semester at FFI, I wrote him letters and sent cards. That was the kind of thing I had done with *The One* because those summers I was at camp we didn't get much phone time. Letters, then, were our breath of life. *The One* wrote back. He sent cards too. He stayed connected to me because he loved me and he wanted me. *Rebound*, not so much.

Mental note.

Rebound had a really rough time that last semester trying to figure out his next step after graduation. It was a dark time for him, and that I understood. I, too, was trying to determine my next step. After college graduation, the expectation is J-O-B, and I had nothing lined up. He didn't either. In fact, he wasn't quite sure what he even wanted to do. His stress became overbearing for him and that became pretty irritating for me. I was a driven student, so if ever there was too much chaos or distraction around me, keeping me from focusing on an academic task or goal, I knew how to tune it all out and laser beam in on my academic pursuits. *Rebound's* indecisiveness and seeming lack of interest in me equaled chaos in my eyes and was becoming quite a distraction, so I officially entered into laser beam mode. I began the signature Iantha tunnel vision that not even a Colorado snowstorm could disrupt, concentrating on nothing but doing well that semester at the Institute. That meant putting *Rebound* on the backburner. I refused to be shaken. If we talked, we talked. If we didn't, we didn't. I didn't have time to figure out what was going on with him or with us when my goal was to ace the four classes I was taking and to hurry up and do it so I could get the heck out of cold, snowy Colorado. I was concerned, at first, with what my roommates thought about how much I talked and didn't talk to this so-called boyfriend of mine, especially because one roommate had a boyfriend back in her home state of Pennsylvania, calling her daily and sending gift after gift to our apartment. That concern dissipated too. I didn't consider their thoughts anymore. I was in my numb stage, and I was strangely pleased with how easy it was to not feel. Since I hadn't ever truly connected to "us," I didn't have to fight to disconnect. He was still my boyfriend, but I felt like we would have to start all over after my semester in Colorado.

Mid-April 2003, after my successful completion of the FFI internship program, I went home to New Orleans, and while there, *Rebound* visited me and my family. Even though I'd talked to my friends and classmates quite a bit about *Rebound*, I hadn't done the same with my family. Sure, they knew about him and were aware that we were "a thing," but they'd always hoped I'd be marrying *The One*. I wasn't sure they were prepared to hear the *Rebound* marriage talk that I'd been sharing with everyone else. Knowing that, I was apprehensive about having him meet my family, but I introduced him to them anyway, trying, still, to recreate something that I was accustomed to with *The One*—the closeness he had with my family. But like everything else I tried to force into existence, it never happened. My family had fallen in love with *The One,* and they were now meeting someone who they couldn't even warm up to. For my family, the memory of *Rebound* quickly faded.

It was soon May and the day of *Rebound's* graduation, so I took the trip to be there. That day, I was with his family for the second time. I'd first met them when I'd surprised him earlier that school year at one of his home games. A friend and I had driven up and gone. After that game, I went out to eat with his family. His sister loved me and I loved her—instant connection. His dad was quiet and a bit indifferent. I knew, immediately upon meeting his mother, that she had high hopes for her son, and I could tell, from the very first time she laid eyes on me, that for her, I wasn't it.

Discernment is a powerful gift, and God had given me an extra dose of it when it came to *Rebound's* mother. Every time I was in her presence, the Holy Spirit gave me the ability to see her thoughts concerning me, so those few times I was around her, I was intentional in making my words few. I sat back, quietly, and listened to the Lord download what He wanted me to know. She wasn't mean or nasty to me, but she wasn't exactly welcoming either.

That night at dinner, after *Rebound's* basketball game, I could see that she prized her son. He was a star player and had much respect on his campus. He had just put on quite a show on the court too. I could see that she'd put a lot into him and that she wasn't allowing some girl she didn't know, who wasn't even a real basketball fan, to have her son and all she'd invested in him. She made such a fuss over him at the dinner table, and I just simply took note.

Graduation day had the same feel. His family knew me because they'd seen me that one time before, but they hadn't, and would never, warm up to me. I was not his future. They saw it, and I had always seen it. I wasn't sure if *Rebound* saw it then, though, because he still talked the same way about us. But soon, he would see it like everyone else had.

The Rebound Recess

Not long after *Rebound's* graduation, I went on to do my last summer at KAA. I didn't talk much to *Rebound*, and I didn't feel compelled to. I had no peace with what was happening with us, and I hadn't had any peace from the very beginning, so I knew "us" couldn't have been what God wanted for me. I took that summer to mentally and spiritually withdraw from the world around me and tune in to God. Completely. Every day, I was seeking Him about *my* life, not about what would happen with *Rebound* and me. I was more concerned about what I would do after camp. Everything in me was sure I wasn't returning to New Orleans because there was a pull inside of me for something more, and that something more was in another place. That, I knew.

One day in my quiet time, after much prayer and study of scripture, I felt led to stop applying for jobs. There was a peace in my heart and in my spirit that comes when I know God is speaking to me, so I knew it was His leading. All summer, although I had no desire to work in journalism, the field in which I'd earned a bachelor's degree, I was sending out resumé after resumé to businesses with positions available for journalists. I was setting up phone interviews galore, trying to secure a job by August. I knew that even if I had to work in a newsroom for a time, I'd be okay until I found what I wanted. But that day, I knew God was telling me to stand still and do nothing else. It was scary, but I trusted Him. I knew He wouldn't tell me to do something and not have me covered. His Word had assured me too many times that He was my guide and that if I trusted Him, I'd never be put to shame.

By that time in my life, I'd developed a deep desire for teaching young women to understand who they are and who they can be in Christ. I'd been teaching girls every summer at camp and loving it, and I'd done some teaching and mentoring through the gospel choir at Tech. During my last quarter at Tech, God placed a heavy burden on my heart for teaching young women and encouraging them, through His Word, to walk in purity in their romantic relationships, and He told me to begin a weekly Bible study in my dorm apartment. The Bible study met every week that quarter, and I knew, from the first meeting, that I'd found the specifics of my purpose; I knew, with everything in me, that I was called to teach young women the Word of God so they could be equipped to not only apply it to their lives, but teach others to as well.

All of the teaching I'd done on purity and abstinence every summer at KAA, with the gospel choir, and through the women's

Bible study was because I was someone who knew what it was like to compromise her purity. I knew I had compromised by not setting boundaries in my relationships, and I knew I didn't set boundaries because I wasn't completely committed to living for God. I knew what it felt like to want to give myself to someone I loved, and I knew the battle that came with knowing I shouldn't. I knew what it felt like to wallow in unhealthy habits that were hard to break. I knew what it was like to struggle with standing strong in the lust battle for a while and then finding myself right back where I started, falling deeper each time than the time before. I knew all about that. God wanted me to reach young women with His love before it got to that with them. He wanted me to teach them how to handle themselves before they even committed to a relationship. He wanted me to teach them to set up boundaries within those relationships so they could progress His way. And since he wanted me to teach young women these things, He created a way for me to do it.

As I was later leaving the dining hall after my quiet time and breakfast to begin the day's schedule, my name was called over the loudspeaker for me to take a phone call in the office. In the weeks before the day God told me to be still and not apply for any jobs, a classmate from FFI had contacted me. She and I hadn't talked much while at FFI, but the few times we did talk, we learned that we both had a passion to teach young women. She knew I had done a Bible study at Tech and that I'd been teaching young women at KAA. She was in Augusta, Georgia with her family, and she'd heard of a company, Heritage Community Services, that was established to teach abstinence in public schools. She applied and got the job and found that the company was looking to hire one more female team member and one male team member. She said she couldn't stop thinking about me and had searched until she found me. After talking to her and praying about the job, I applied when God gave me the okay to do so. That job possibility had spoken to my heart like no other one had all summer. It's what I wanted, and honestly, what I knew *He* wanted for me. God's telling me to be still was His way of removing distractions for me to hear that opportunity clearly. Nothing else was there to compete with the one thing that He wanted me to see. It still blows my mind today!

When I got to the phone, the voice on the other end was the director of the program. She'd gotten my application and resumé and wanted to talk more. We entered into a phone interview, and by the end of the interview, which was more like a conversation, I was hired! I was a slobbery, tearful mess for the rest of the day. Grateful. Humbled. In total awe of God!

When camp was over in a month or so after that call, I headed to New Orleans to pack up and moved to Augusta to start my young adult life.

The Rebound Wrap-Up

That night, when I came off of my cloud, I was reminded of something: *Rebound* had family in Georgia that I later learned wasn't too far from Augusta. That turned my attention back to our possibilities. I wondered, for a moment, if "we" could work, but that was shut down in a jiff with the ever-present truth that I had no real peace about us. I knew where I was headed. I wasn't moving to Georgia because *Rebound* could possibly end up there after his post-graduation internship. I was moving there because God commissioned me there. I couldn't wait to spend intimate, undisturbed time in prayer and fasting to know what He wanted me to do on "my assignment" in my new set place. I knew I was called to a pool of young women that I had yet to meet, so I didn't need confusion. I didn't need uncertainty. I didn't need distractions. *Rebound* didn't know what He wanted. He had no clue what was going on with his life at that point, and I wasn't about to get mixed up in that.

I moved to Augusta in late August 2003, and by mid-September, God had told me to turn *Rebound* over to Him. He needed *Rebound* all to Himself. I didn't need to be in his ear and I didn't want to be. He needed to figure things out for himself. I wasn't comfortable with any thought of "us" because if *Rebound* was planning to lead us as a married unit, he needed, first, to know what he was doing with himself. So we took time apart and went on a full-blown hiatus. The confines of our time apart was zero communication—no phone calls, no texts, no emails. I told him to contact me when he felt God told him to, and when he felt he had a grip on where the Lord was leading Him. We agreed that he shouldn't even think about reaching out to me if he didn't. I had no problem giving *Rebound* over to the Lord. I was ready to drop it all right there if God had said so. He needed that time, as a man, to get his feet on the ground and to not have to worry about how he was going to take care of a wife too. More than anything, because I cared about him, I just wanted to see him at peace.

I told him, "Just do you. If when you contact me, you're ready, okay. If when you contact me, you're not, and we decide to do other things, cool."

Months went by, and as the new year settled in, *Rebound* contacted me via email. I knew he wasn't *my* man then. He didn't want me, and that was totally fine. In the email, he told me to call him if I wanted to talk about the things he'd written. He also said he would understand if I didn't want to talk. But I definitely wanted to talk. I didn't want to leave room for assumption. I followed up a couple days later with a phone call because a conversation was necessary. Even though in the email he'd danced around what he really wanted to say, it was clear that he wanted me to be the one to say we should end things, so I did. After addressing some of the specifics in the email, I ended it, and I wasn't the least bit sad. God had my heart.

Plus, according to my journal, in November, I had moved on in my mind anyway. I had determined then that…

He wasn't it either.

Rebound Real Talk

Oh, what sadness to be untrue to oneself
and live a lie.

***Rebound Real Talk #1 – When you're experiencing the hurt that
sometimes comes with a breakup, go to the Lord. Spend time
alone with God instead of jumping into another relationship.***

I didn't realize I was attempting to mask my pain after the
breakup with *The One* by continuing on with life as if nothing had
happened. I was not okay. I was hurting. Badly. But I didn't even
give myself time to see the hurt, let alone process and heal from it.
My whole reason for ending things with *The One* was to honor
God with my whole heart, so if that was the case, why didn't I run
to Him? Why didn't I lay my hurt and pain at His feet?

Psalm 34:18 (NIV) says, *"The Lord is close to the
brokenhearted and saves those who are crushed in spirit."* I didn't
allow the Lord to be close to my broken heart and my crushed
spirit. I didn't allow him to comfort and refresh me. I didn't allow
Him to build me up in His presence and in His Word, but that
doesn't have to be the case for you. If you experience a painful
breakup, run to the Lord and be alone with Him for however long
it takes for you to be completely healed from the pain. You will
need to be restored. You will need time to refocus and regroup,
especially if the relationship was a courtship that was heading
toward marriage. You won't be in a place to healthily give of
yourself to someone else.

God blew my mind with everything He showed me once I
finally gave Him my broken heart. I could hear His voice so
clearly! He showed me the hurt and how I had been trying to mask
it. He showed me that my relationship with *Rebound* was, in fact, a
rebound relationship. The best part, though, was how He began to
show me the specifics of why He'd called me to Augusta. He
finally had my full attention, and He'd been trying to get it since
I'd broken up with *The One*. That's all God wanted. He wanted to
give me some new strategies for making disciples. I needed to

reestablish my purpose, and I wouldn't have heard it as clearly, or maybe even at all, if I didn't tune completely in to the Lord.

I caution you, if you *do* jump into another relationship without allowing the Lord time to heal you, you run the risk of experiencing even more pain because you'll be exposing your wound to possible infection. When an open wound becomes infected because it doesn't get the type of attention it needs to heal properly, the infection can cause even bigger problems in the body, and that slows down the healing process. It could get so bad that an amputation may be necessary because a part of the body that was perfectly normal before the wound was inflicted is no longer even functional. Don't let that be you. Don't cause the Lord to have to cut you to get your attention. Allow Him to begin your healing process at the onset of the pain.

Rebound Real Talk #2 – Just because he wants to get with you doesn't mean you have to let him. Be selective.

Every woman who's had a few male suitors in her life can think of a time when she gave her phone number to someone she knew wasn't worthy of her time or when she entertained a guy she wasn't genuinely interested in. Why do we do this? Why do we give our attention to gentlemen simply because they ask for it? And why do we feel like we have to "be nice" or humor them just because they have a decent approach? I wish we would take the time to be more thoughtfully selective.

When *Rebound* came along, I wasn't even in the position to think clearly because I was aching from the pain of my open wound. The questions I needed to ask him up front, I was too spacey to even think about asking. I let him do most of the talking, and because I was numb, I just went along with it. He said we should get together, and I went with it. He started talking marriage, and I went with it. None of it ever felt right, but I never stopped the proceeding. I just gave in. I had every right to say I wasn't diggin' him. I had every right to say I wasn't feelin' what was going on, even if he was 100% with it. Just because he wanted to be with me didn't mean I had to let him. I had every right to be selective. And, ladies, you need to know that you do too. You need to know that it's okay to leave him right where he stands if (1) you know you're not genuinely interested in him, (2) he's not someone you can see yourself "working" with, and (3) there's no purposeful connection. And know, too, that you don't have to "be nice" just to appease or humor him.

If I would've taken a little more time to just talk to *Rebound* like someone who was in pursuit of me instead of still treating him like my brother and friend (*because that's two very different conversations*), I would've known very soon that we weren't compatible. I could've easily cut things off before they even got started. Had I done that, instead of trying to continue "being nice" to my friend, we wouldn't have wasted each other's time. I would've known that I wasn't genuinely interested in him, that he wasn't someone I wanted to "work" with, and that we had no purposeful connection.

So, I say to you, it's okay to let suitors pass you by. Not everyone who tries to "holla at you" is someone you should connect with. Not everyone who asks for your time is worthy of it. If you know you're not genuinely interested, for God's sake, don't lead him on. Be true to you. If you know he's going to be a waste of your time, don't allow him in your space. If you know you're not compatible, don't try to make it so. You know when you know it's not right. Leave it there.

Rebound Real Talk #3 – Decisions made in haste are usually disastrous. What's the rush?

God's Word speaks about how disastrous hasty decisions can be. Proverbs 21:5 (NIV) says, *"The plans of the diligent lead to profit as surely as haste leads to poverty."* This verse is speaking specifically about the right and wrong way to gain wealth, but it can certainly be applied in other areas. I was able to see how this principle can speak to relationships, especially, when I read it in The Message (MSG) version. It says, *"Careful planning puts you ahead in the long run; hurry and scurry puts you further behind."*

It's true. Think about it this way...

When a house is being built, it's important for a solid, strong foundation to be laid first because the house needs it to be able to stand. If there isn't a strong foundation, the house may stand for a while, but eventually, it will begin to shift and experience all the problems that come along with that. It may even collapse. This is why the builder can't be in too much of a hurry to get to the final product. The builder has to spend time securing a firm foundation, no matter how long it takes. The same is true for relationships. A solid, firm foundation has to be in place, and that takes time.

If a man is hasty about anything in the relationship, that's cause for caution. **STOP** and pay attention. The haste can be an indication that he is insecure and "needs" what he "needs" to fill a void. It could be a sign that he's hiding something. It could be that he's lustful and just wants to have sex. There are endless "could be's" but regardless of the reason, it should not go without your thorough examination. Take the time to talk through things at length with him.

And get to know who he is when he's with different people—friends, family, coworkers. How do they see him, and what do they know about him? Make it your business to see him in different seasons and situations. How does he handle stress? How does he handle success? What is he like when he's angry? You should, at the absolute least, see all of these things before you yield to marriage exclusivity.

Rushing is the reddest red light ever! Don't be hasty in your dating, and don't allow him to be.

Rebound Real Talk #4 – Actions speak louder than words.

- When a man wants to be with you, he doesn't leave you guessing; he makes it clear that with you is where he wants to be.
- When a man wants to be with you, the last thing he wants you to think is that he *doesn't* want to be with you. He'll work overtime to make sure that doesn't happen.
- When a man wants to be with you, he refuses to run the risk of losing you. He knows if his actions don't consistently say he wants to be with you, he can lose you, and he's not letting that happen. He knows a woman worth having won't allow him to say he wants to be with her and not show it. He knows his actions have to speak much louder than his words, so he makes his actions do all the talking.

In the beginning of our relationship, *Rebound* showed me that he wanted to be with me. There was no question about his intentions for me. It was later during my Colorado semester that he had me guessing. It was like he was a totally different person. During that time, I often wondered, *So, wait… Are we even still doing this?* Imagine what it must feel like to have someone, for months, going over the top to let you know just how into you they are and then, all of a sudden, they fall back. Wouldn't that "action" speak pretty loudly to you? Why was I the only one concerned about us seeing each other while I was in Colorado? Why was he not making an effort? Why was phone conversation suddenly not as important to him? Why were we going days without talking? I went through shock, you hear me? I was used to a man *wanting* to be in my space because he *wanted* to be with me, and that wasn't happening. Because I knew what it looked and felt like to be desired, I could see when I wasn't, and I didn't care about the words he said whenever we talked; I was watching his actions.

You won't have to wonder if he's into you when he really wants to be with you. Did you hear me? I said you won't have to wonder if he's into you when he really wants to be with you.

Rebound Real Talk #5 – A man needs time to figure himself out. Give him that time.

The greatest gift you can ever give a man is time to himself—alone—to figure things out. If you see he's struggling with knowing what to do with his life, he's not ready to be with you. If he can't figure himself out, he certainly won't be able to figure himself out in a relationship. Care enough about him to give him to the Lord, the only one who can get his life in order. And when you give him over to the Lord, step away. Completely. If there was something between the two of you worth keeping, it won't go anywhere. If there wasn't, then congratulations! You dodged a bullet.

Rebound Real Talk #6 – Compatibility is necessary.

Are there some things that the two of you can enjoy together that have nothing to do with God?

Yes, I just asked that question!

Do you?

If you are in relationship with God through Jesus Christ, Jesus will be the cornerstone (Ha! Bible thumpin'!) of that relationship. Ain't no gettin' around that. He will inevitably be intertwined in everything you do, but there is more to you than just your relationship with Him. You don't live your life, 24 hours a day, lying prostrate before the Lord. No one does. God gave you gifts and talents that more than likely formed your hobbies and interests, and if you're human, which I'm sure you are, you indulge in those hobbies and interests. You still enjoy the things that bring you happiness and fulfillment outside of your relationship with the

Lord, don't you? And what a tragedy if you can't enjoy those things with the person you're in relationship with!

I didn't enjoy *Rebound* as a boyfriend. I couldn't connect with him. As friends, we could talk about God all day because we didn't have to connect to do that. I wasn't thinking about spending the rest of my life with him so we were able to talk and leave it there. When I was considering being with him, though, I wanted to talk freely about my life and my interests and have effortless conversation. That wasn't happening with us; it was too much work.

If the person you're dating doesn't, at minimum, show appreciation for the things you're interested in (and vice versa), you two may not be compatible. If it's like pulling teeth when you're out together trying to do something fun, you're probably not compatible. If your conversations never click, and if it's like a job trying to have a conversation about anything other than Jesus, you're probably not compatible, and the relationship won't work. There's no reason you should set yourself up to date someone you can't hang out with, and you certainly don't want to consider marrying anyone you can't have fun with. You have to be able to enjoy each other outside of church. Refuse the unnecessary labor.

Rebound Real Talk #7 – Physical attraction matters.

One thing I've always said to my friends about my one-day husband is I have to *want* to make babies with him. And guess what? I'm sure he will want the same. We can love God all day, and spiritual attraction carries a lot of weight, for sure, but, honey, when it's time for physical intimacy, we probably won't be praying and singing worship songs. Our spiritual attraction will more than likely be the last thing on our minds.

Don't lie to yourself like I did and say, "He's not my kinda cute, but…" or "I'm not marrying his flesh; I'm marrying his spirit." I'm glad I wised up. I'll be marrying my husband's spirit that resides in a fleshly shell that is pleasing to my senses. And I promise you he wants to do the same.

Rebound Real Talk #8 – Be honest with yourself. The peace in your heart, or lack thereof, is your measuring stick. That peace is God's greatest gift to you.

Too often, ladies, we try to *make* things work. We'll suppress our feelings and tell ourselves that something isn't there when it clearly is, staring us right in the face. Or we'll tell ourselves that something is there when it isn't. We'll say something didn't hurt our feelings because we want to keep the peace. We'll rearrange our schedules, cut appointments, stay out later than we need to, wake up earlier than we want to, and a heap of other things that we wouldn't normally do for the sake of making something work that we can clearly see isn't working.

Your spirit is steadily screaming, telling you to speak up, but you silence it and you keep smiling and playing along. You're uncomfortable every time he says something about how stupid he thinks church is, and you shudder when you see him buy liquor, but you push it aside as something that you can change about him if you just hang in there with him a little while longer. Been there, done that. Haven't changed one yet, and I *won't* change any. The truth is this: You know very early on, maybe even upon just meeting the guy, if he's worthy of your time. There are things he says, and there are things he does that you can see don't line up with who you are. Don't push past those red lights. Don't silence the sirens. Those are the things that are rattling God's peace in your heart. Those "shake ups" are your ticket out. Get out before you're too entangled. If you're uncomfortable, there's a reason. Don't ignore it. You have to be honest with yourself. Don't try to make it work if it ain't workin'.

I hung around with *Rebound* because I was clinging to "the man of God" image. I knew he loved God, so everything else I'd have to just learn to deal with. Nope! That's not how it works. Now, don't get me wrong. There are things about a person that are negotiable like maybe he smacks his food, or he lets a toothpick hang out of his mouth while he talks, or he pops his knuckles whenever he's nervous. Those are quirks. We all have them. When you marry, you marry quirks. Those are the things that wise married women of God will tell you that you just have to accept because he'll be accepting yours too. But things that are beyond quirks, like he doesn't study the Word of God or live a life that pleases Him… Those are *foundational warning signs* that pull at the peace in your heart. You don't need to ignore them.

Rebound Real Talk #9 – Family relationships are important.

I've seen when my family approved of someone that my siblings, cousins, or I brought home, and I've seen when my family disapproved of someone. I'm fonder of what it looks like when my family approves because when they do, there's peace and harmony. When they don't, there's tension and discomfort. And this is because my family (and most families) understands that when someone is that much a part of our lives (exclusive relationship) there is no way they can be with us and not be connected to our family. It's impossible.

I saw this evidenced best when I was in middle school and my brother brought my sister-in-law home to meet my parents, my sister, and me. Our entire family had an immediate connection with her, and over the years, it has only grown stronger. My parents embraced her as their own; she's their daughter. She instantly became my sister, and to this day, I talk to her more than I talk to my own brother and sister. We just have that kind of relationship. And if I can't have that type of oneness with the family of the man I plan to marry, that's not the family I want to marry into.

The Lord spoke to me clearly to show me all of the areas that *Rebound's* mom didn't approve of concerning me. He also showed me how my family didn't approve of *Rebound* for me. My family knew that we weren't God's best for each other. God assured me that *Rebound's* family wouldn't love me the way He would have me to be loved in my marriage. He reminded me of what I'd seen in my own family and urged me to not settle for anything less. And now I urge you.

You've probably heard people say, "I'm not marrying his/her family. I'm marrying him/her."

LIE!

You *are* marrying his family because you're marrying *into* his family. When have you ever known anyone to completely disconnect from their family? Even if they say they're breaking ties with their family, there's no way to be completely disconnected. Some type of familial connection will surface at some point or another. It's inevitable. You want to do your best to make sure you have peace with the family of the one to whom you're committing.

I'm just crazy enough to believe that when God approves of a relationship (marriage), he pulls families together in peace. Now, of course there are always exceptions. There may be some cases where things work out just fine regardless of what's happening with the families involved, but for the most part, families know when someone is good for their children. Most times, those on the outside can see what we can't, so if your family expresses disapproval, don't ignore it. At least explore it.

Tweet your takeaways from *Rebound*.
#HWIERebound

If it resonated with you,
it can probably help someone else.

Tag me in your posts on Twitter and Instagram.

Let's connect!

@ianthasinsight

From the Outside Looking In: A Word from Iantha's Best Friend

We were made in the image of God. This means that the ability to relate and be in community with God first, then others, is a beautifully wondrous thing. But just like all things that began in perfection, sin distorted how relationships work. Sin first wreaked our relationship with God, thus making it that much harder to be in relationship with others, especially relationships with the opposite sex and relationships within the Body of Christ. But praise be to God for not leaving us "to' up from the flo' up" in our relationship with Him!

God, in His mercy, sent Jesus Christ, who knew no sin, to become sin so you and I could be in right relationship with God. And once right with God, we can learn to be in community with one another.

This newfound ability to be in community isn't easy, y'all, especially amongst believers. See, though sin no longer controls us, we still have this pesky sin nature that wants us to return to old habits passed down from the first humans, Adam and Eve. One of these habits is believing the lie that we must hide from God, or as I like to put it, "front as if we have it all together". This hiding from God will also cause us to hide from the community we were meant to thrive in, and Satan loves when we isolate ourselves from the safety that community provides. It's open season for him.

When you're not honest about what you are dealing with as you work out your salvation and press your way through sanctification, you give the enemy room to make you feel as if you are the only one on the struggle bus with whatever has you bound. Satan will choke you with your silence and have you living on the fringes of a glorious faith walk with Jesus. Even worse, the enemy wants those who've never surrendered to Christ to continue hiding from God, crouched and covered in shame, believing they somehow can escape His presence and are unworthy of His love.

If you are the one hiding, can I tell you that God, your Creator, the Lover of your soul and all that you are, desires to have a relationship with you? You don't need to pretend to have it all together. Whether you are a believer struggling under the weight of hidden sin or an unbeliever pulled down by the penalty of sin, know that all you need to do is be honest about where you are (He already knows anyway), and confess your sin that you may walk in forgiveness, power and community.

Community is awesome! I praise God for it every day. Without my community of strong women and men in the faith, I would not be able to push against the current of this world. Nope! And God didn't intend for me to do so. That is why He allowed me to have an Iantha, someone who I can fight this battle with (*you know you are in a war, right?*), who will have my back, who will cry with me, and who will challenge me and sometimes just be with me. I have had the privilege of watching Iantha's life in Christ grow and mature into what it is today. Many a night we sat on the phone processing scripture or praying over some of the relationship situations that she details in this book. There were times I would yell out, "Girl, this will help a woman some day!" I believed it with everything in me, and I still do. There is no way in the world that God would allow my best friend and accountability partner to persevere in what is complicated, messy and mystifying without it producing a testimony that would help others overcome.

God has given Iantha a poignant, laser-focused, unwavering word for us in the pages of this book. And I say "us" because we are a community. Hello! I'm so glad you're here. Iantha has laid herself bare so God can be glorified while we discover tools to help us heal from unhealthy relationships, and walk in healthy relationships with men. Just like Eve, Iantha hid from the truth of what was really happening in her heart regarding the men in the pages to follow. She tried to fix things up and "make it make sense," but God's fierce love for her brought her out of that darkness and into the liberating light. I believe it wasn't just God's love for Iantha that wouldn't allow her to continue hiding, but His love for YOU, Beloved. He wants you to worship Him in truth, and sometimes hearing someone else's story helps. We are meant to grow and learn through shared experiences of God's amazing grace. That's what community is all about! Hallelujah!

So, as you turn the page, know that there are women everywhere joining with you. As a few of your toes get stepped on, know that we are all sucking in our breath. When you say "Amen," somebody is saying "Ouch." And when you put this book down to take a breath because the truth is slapping you in the face, know that you have a great crowd of witnesses, past and present, urging you to continue seeking truth and thereby, freedom. You are not alone. You never were. You'll see.

Chantel Mack

The Secret

Shhh…

I'm gonna take my time with this one, ladies.

After it was clear that the door was slammed shut on *Rebound* forever, I went on the ride of my life with Jesus. With my newly untethered heart and mind and sure sense of freedom, all I wanted was to get direction from God on how to make disciples. I knew He wanted me to pour myself into teaching, guiding, and encouraging young ladies to walk in His ways; He had already made that crystal clear before I even planted my feet on Augusta soil. My primary concern then, every day, was seeking the Lord in prayer and in His Word so I could know who, specifically, to reach and how to reach them. And as I sought Him, He surely revealed. Not a day lapsed that God wasn't giving me some vision, some idea, or some plan for me to complete my mission. At the same time, He was telling me how I should handle myself in dating relationships, even though dating was the farthest thing from my mind. I was definitely taking my time. It would be a couple of years before I would entertain even a compliment from a man. I was *that* focused and content. But God didn't hold back during that time. He rolled out His instructions before me one day in my prayer time, and in the quiet of my heart, I received two directives: *(1) Do not entertain anyone in my home, and do not accept invites to any of my suitors' homes, and (2) Do not initiate anything with any man—conversation, setting up a date—nothing*, which was never my style anyway. I'm super old-fashioned in that respect. Throughout those first few years in Augusta, I did what the Lord told me to do with the couple of guys who showed interest in me. Then one night at an event my church was hosting, I messed it all up.

The Secret and I attended different churches, but our congregations joined together pretty often to worship, to serve in the community, and to fellowship, and it was one of those nights. The worship service had ended, and as was customary after any service, fellowship was in full bloom in the vestibule. It was not uncommon for the congregants to stand and discuss, for quite a stretch of time, what we'd just received from the Word of God or to just talk life in general. Whatever the case, hardly anyone ever went straight home. *The Secret* had a routine of posting himself in one spot. He wasn't one to navigate through the myriad of intimate circles that pervaded the space. He wasn't one to etch himself into conversations that were already underway. He usually allowed a small circle of his own to form with him as the nucleus, and the circle was almost always exclusively made up of teen boys. That night was no different. Before long, the little cell of maybe three or four guys evolved into a bulging huddle. When I walked by the huddle with a few of the girls who'd become my mentees, we joined the guys and learned that the crowd had gathered for more than just talking; *The Secret* was distributing brownies and cookies. Kids seemed to rush out of nowhere and from everywhere at the same time, which made it hard to believe that after many attempts to rid himself of the last few sweet treats, he hadn't managed to do so. *The Secret* just about begged me to have some of what was left so he wouldn't have to eat it all himself, but I told him, after thanking him for the offer, that I wasn't in the mood for sweets. Then the strangest thing happened. My declination seemed to magically transpose itself into an invitation for him to relentlessly insist. It was crazy! And he was pouring it on pretty thick.

With a sheepish grin spread across his face, he urged, "C'mon, now. You know you want one." His eyes went from an excited brightness to a relaxed puppy-dog pleading. Gently, but dismissively, I gave a final "No, thank you. I'm good," and redirected my attention to the teens in what had gone from a mellow huddle to a sugar-infused, exuberant horde.

After all of the goodies were finally gone, the crowd dispersed and I went to chat with one of my dear friends who is still, to this day, like a big sister. With literally every other person in the church that night being engaged in some conversation or rap session, she somehow managed to be standing alone. I don't think I'll ever know if her solo stance was one of cunning premeditation or if the stars just happened to align that way for that moment, but as I walked toward her, the impatient expression on her face told me everything I needed to know. I instantly took notice that she had been only a few feet away from that huddle. I hadn't paid it any attention before, but realizing it then, I also discerned that she, the big sister that she is, had probably witnessed the exchange between *The Secret* and me. Within seconds of standing face to face with her, she confirmed my notion.

With her teeth clenched, and her eyes peering directly into mine, she spoke in a low tone and said, "Iantha, he is *flir-ting* with you. *Why-ee* didn't you just take a brownie?"

It was as if I had failed a test she'd spent weeks preparing me for, like she couldn't believe I hadn't chosen the right answers after we'd reviewed the exact test questions time and time again. Although she hadn't coached me on how to date or what to look for, or any other Relationship 101isms, she had an endearing nature that showed itself every now and then. She loved me, and she wanted me to have true love with someone. It was one of those unspoken cheerleader moments for her, when she didn't have to say that she'd hoped a connection would be made with *The Secret* and me, but she allowed everything she said behind what she didn't say to say it for her.

After her mini scolding session, she relaxed her tightened jaws. Her eyes softened. She even took a step back to create a comfortable space between us. Then, with the familiar gentleness in her voice that I was accustomed to, she shared some final words with me. She said, "Sometimes you just have to help them out a little bit. He's trying really hard to talk to you."

In my heart, I knew if *The Secret* wanted to get more conversation from me than what our usual exchanges at church had offered or if he wanted to ask me out, he should initiate it. God had made that very clear to me. I thought to myself, *I'm not helping him ask me for more conversation, and I'm not helping him ask me out. He needs to open up his mouth and say that's what he wants if that's what he wants.* But nestled behind that thought was the nagging reminder of my friend's words, "Sometimes you just have to help them out a little bit…" It hadn't been the first time she'd said that. And it hadn't been the first time she'd said it, specifically, about him.

…And Again

That next night, the final session of the two-night event, the service ended as it always did—with clusters of people in fellowship. *The Secret* surprisingly somehow found his way to me after breaking free from his gaggle of guys, and for a spell, we engaged in the ho-hum small talk that he and I had grown accustomed to. I wasn't naïve. I could see he was flirting. The brownies weren't the first time he'd tried to weasel his way near me; the brownies weren't the first time he couldn't carry on any real conversation; the brownies weren't the first time he'd have to hurry and look away when my eyes traveled in his direction. By that time, though, on *that* night, with the extra added pressure of hearing my friend in the back of my mind, I kept thinking to myself, *Why won't he just spit it out?* I don't even remember what he was saying while we were standing there in that congested foyer. I do remember, however, how I could see him searching his mental Rolodex for words to say to me while he had me all to himself for that moment. He knew, like I knew, that the moment was sure to soon be snatched away by the teens. And that's exactly what happened, but it came with an advantageous crutch for him.

They mobbed us. All the teens surrounded us with their non-stop bolts of energy and started talking about a movie that had just come out. A few of them were talking about how good the movie was, and others, after hearing the reviews, talked about how they were definitely going to see it. *The Secret* looked beyond a couple of the kids that stood between us, and when his eyes finally met mine, he asked if I'd seen the movie. I said, "No. I haven't, actually. Why? Are we going to see it?"

His eyes widened with disbelief and he just stared at me. A smile crept across his face and planted itself there while his mind, I could tell, tried to formulate intelligible words. But he was speechless. I'd caught him off guard. He did eventually follow up with something that I don't quite remember, but I knew immediately that I'd regret having "helped him out a little bit" because that was the exact kind of initiating that the Lord told me to steer clear of.

The Secret had chocolate brown skin. He was average height, and his build bore a strong resemblance to the record producer, songwriter, and artist, Pharrell Williams. He had perfectly round eyes that smiled when he smiled his big white smile. Those eyes would widen when he was excited, and they'd soften when he was in a good mood. It was easy to tell when he was serious or engaged in a really good conversation because then his eyes would squint a little with intentness. And when he wanted to speak with that tone that was designed to let a woman know he desired her, his eyes would relax to just about closed and glare with purpose.

He walked with a heaviness, like his weight was too much on his feet, but it wasn't pounds that weighed him down. It was his quiet disposition that made him so dense. He was hard to read, and it kept him hidden in plain sight. He seemed, too, to always have on clothes—a jacket or an oversized baseball jersey or too-big jeans or all of them at once—that helped his walk seem even heavier. His shoulders slouched a bit with his steps, and his head dropped a little too, but it wasn't a slouch or drop of the head that a hunchback would don. It didn't look uncomfortable or painful in his case. Strangely, his heaviness would sort of glide when he walked, and the wonder in that was a drawing card for me. Just like a secret treasure box, when one is dying to know what's inside, *The Secret* had that kind of mystery. No one really knew much about its contents, and without a key, there was no getting in.

There was nothing overly attractive about him, but he definitely wasn't unattractive. His intrigue, alone, piqued my interest, but it didn't hurt that he was well-groomed and had a decent relationship with cologne. I don't think I would've been able to "help him out a little bit" without all of that being in tow.

I don't remember how we exchanged numbers. I don't remember if we even went to see that movie. What I do remember, though, is that things changed almost instantly after that moment.

Rules of Engagement

You see, before there was ever anything between *The Secret* and me, and we'd find ourselves in each other's company, we would stop and talk just as we would with anyone else, and just as we'd done those two nights at my church. But when we became "a thing," that was no more. It was as if a heavy curtain had instantly been pulled to cover us, and anything we said or did from that moment forward was always behind that curtain. No one saw "us" out in the open, and except for three people *The Secret* and I both considered friends, no one would ever see "us" as we were. From the start, he wanted me to be his secret, and although he never overtly said that was the case, the message was hard to miss whenever we were together. I didn't know that's what I was getting into because it's certainly not what I signed up for, but after a few months in, I looked up, and there I was—in the dark—hiding with *The Secret*.

Throughout the first few weeks of getting to know each other, *The Secret* and I talked on the phone some, but we mostly texted. When we *did* talk on the phone, we didn't talk like people who wanted to get to know each other beyond our already-established church relationship. Not at first anyway. The phone conversations during those first few weeks were pretty much always at surface level, just as they'd always been at church, and for someone like me, who loathes small talk, I had already had enough of that after the second night of the church event. I was being uncommonly polite with him—well past my usual allotment—until I just couldn't do it anymore. I knew *The Secret* wasn't calling and texting like he was to just be my church buddy, so I started asserting myself to make my expectations clear for what I believed was happening between us.

In one pretty candid conversation, I told *The Secret* I needed him to respect my peace. I explained to him that I was at an amazing place of peace in my life and in my walk with the Lord. I told him I wanted, more than anything, to remain in that peace. In fact, I took the liberty of describing what peace looked like and didn't look like for me. I explained that if he was carrying drama from any past relationships or was still somehow connected to women from any of his past relationships, we could do what we had been doing—talking at church. I told him I would not have women whom he once dated, approaching me, confronting me, or anything of the sort to ask questions or quench their curiosity about my dealings with him. I let him know if anything like that happened even one time, he wouldn't be granted a moment to explain. I'd seen too many incidents and heard too many horror stories, and I wasn't interested in having any of my own. I prided myself in making sure that when I ended a relationship with someone, there was no miscommunication about our being over and done. I issued what I call "clean cuts," making it very clear that there was no chance for a reconnection. I assured *The Secret* that he could rest in knowing my past was buried. I thought it only fair for me to have the same consideration and respect. That, to me, equaled peace.

I also expressed my need for honesty. I told him I wanted to be able to trust what he said. I didn't have trust issues in any of the relationships I'd had in my life up to that point, and I didn't want to start having any. I let *The Secret* know that if he couldn't tell me the truth and be open and honest, we didn't need to be together. I didn't want to have to wonder about him or about us because that, to me, wasn't peaceful. I ended my spiel by boldly declaring that I was fine before he had come along and if he was going to disrupt that, he could leave me be. He assured me he understood.

I had obviously opened up the door for us to begin talking about what was really happening with us because in that same conversation, *The Secret* seemed to finally feel comfortable enough to tell me how he felt about me. He told me I was like a craving, which I thought was a pretty clever way for him to explain how someone like me was what he had always wanted, but how he didn't really know it until I showed up. In his eyes, and in his words, I was perfect, and as time progressed, he would tell me I was the kind of perfect that made it hard for him to wrap his mind around. Often, he would tell me I was too good to be true, and he would always point out the qualities in me that made it seem so. He liked that I was college-educated and independent and that I loved the Lord and served faithfully in church. He didn't miss an opportunity to tell me I was beautiful. He liked that I worked out and didn't drink, smoke, or go out to clubs, and he praised my thoughtfulness and the fact that others spoke highly of me. But in the same breath, with the same tongue he used to speak well of me, he would roll out the dark clouds and cast a shadow over himself by saying things like, "How could someone like me have managed to get time with someone like you?" and "How did you get to be so perfect?" It appeared he felt like he didn't measure up to me, and for the life of me, I couldn't see why he felt that way since he was a successful entrepreneur and one heck of a business man. But the Holy Spirit helped me see things clearly.

After some time, by the Lord's leading, I eventually saw *The Secret's* "sing her praises and doubt myself" act for what it really was. By regularly expressing that he felt like he would never be able to measure up, it was his hope that I would never expect him to. And not that he had to be exactly who I was or do what I'd done, but in his thinking, if he could look like he didn't have enough to offer in the relationship, then he'd never really have to offer anything. If things went his way, he wouldn't ever have to be fully present in the relationship because, hopefully, I'd be thinking he wasn't capable of that. The relationship, then, would never get too serious because he would never quite get to where he needed to be for it to work. It was such a player move, but the Lord uncovered that tactic and would reveal more in time.

Anatomy of the Secret

The Secret worked three different jobs, something I knew upon first meeting him through his family members that attended my church. Two of the three jobs were his businesses. I'd actually seen him in action on all three jobs, so at the very beginning of our time together, I was respectful   that. He was a grown man. He had a life and responsibilities. I didn't press. I wasn't trying to keep him from doing what he needed to do for his livelihood, but for us, that meant he never had time until *he* had time so *he* was ultimately in control of when we got together and where we went whenever we did get together. I knew there were days when he worked from sun up to sundown and would try to make time for us. I saw the times when he appeared to genuinely try, and I let him know I appreciated it, but after some time, again, by way of the Holy Spirit, I could see something more. Although those three jobs were legitimate reasons for him being as distant as he was, he used it to his advantage to be able to "travel in the dark" whenever he wanted to. He liked it that way. He liked that there was never really any time in his schedule so he wouldn't have to commit to too much or try to make too much happen with us. He wasn't trying to hide, but he wasn't *not* trying to hide either. He rode that "always busy with work" bus until the wheels fell off; there was no doubt about it. He knew the less time he spent with me, the smaller the chances were for me to see what he was really about, and there would be less likelihood of a true connection.

We, of course, saw each other most Sundays or whenever anything else was going on at either of our churches, but as I said, after we decided to take things outside of the church, we hardly even acknowledged each other in the church setting anymore. During that first month or so, I was actually cool with not being seen together any differently than we had been before. We barely even knew each other. We were figuring things out, and the last thing we needed was to blab about our being together when we didn't even know if we *were* together. *The Secret* expressed, pretty vehemently, that he thought it would be best for us to lay low for a little bit. A few times he said, "People are nosey, and especially at church. I just don't want people all in our business like that." And I went along with that until going along with it became suspiciously uncomfortable.

After our first few months of "being together," we went from seeing each other only at church to hanging out outside of those four walls. From casual talk to morning phone calls. From church buddy texts to texts that discussed more than friendship. From a few calls a week to making it our business to speak with one another before each day ended. It was apparent there was more to what we had going on than just getting to know each other. In fact, most of our conversations were about us being in an exclusive relationship, so it didn't make sense for us to walk by each other on any given Sunday at church and not acknowledge that we'd just spoken on the phone an hour or so prior. But that's what we were doing, and that was only a fraction of the craziness. There was nothing more disheartening or suspiciously uncomfortable than him and me, on several occasions, being at a mutual friend's house at the same time, trying our best to always be in different spaces so people wouldn't "read us" and know we were more than what they'd known us to be. It was absolute foolishness. And it was confusing. When had that unspoken rule even begun with us? When had I signed a contract agreeing to keep us behind that dark curtain that, clearly, *he* had drawn on us? At times, it was just down right hurtful. My peace was officially shaken, so I knew it was time to start talking about where "our thing" was going. At that point, there was absolutely no reason things should have still been on the hush, and I wasn't going for it anymore.

My tone and attitude started to change whenever we talked. I was annoyed with the here-and-there, dead-end conversations. Making time for us in his days seemed to become stressful for him, and when I began demanding that I at least know his intentions for me and our "relationship," he shied away and rerouted conversations, sometimes completely avoiding them. I kept wondering, *If the pressure is too much and he can't answer questions about us, why is he hanging around? Why does he even bring up relationship talk when he can't definitively say if he even wants a relationship?*

I was exhausted with just trying to figure out what was going on with us. I was tired of walking on eggshells around the events in my own life too. I hadn't been talking freely with anyone in my circle of trust about what was going on with me, and I refused to continue going on that way. I'd never lived my life behind closed doors, and I wasn't about to start. So, one day, in one of our dead-end conversations, I told *The Secret* that I was ready to end whatever it was we had going on. I told him I was checking out because I hadn't signed up to be strung along. I hopped right off of the secret rollercoaster I'd been on so I could keep my peace intact.

He was shocked.

The next few days after my surprise farewell were interesting, to say the least. The barrage of text messages was unreal. There was no begging or pleading, but there was a lot of "I'm sorry" and even more of "I'd like a chance to make it right." All I really wanted was for *The Secret* to man up and say he didn't want a relationship because I knew he didn't, even if sometimes he may have acted like he did. At the same time, though, I was a little curious to see if those text messages could hold their weight. Against my better judgement, I responded with a "yes" to one of the many requests for him to "make it right," and that "yes" became our first official date. I wanted to see if anything would change, and I wanted to see if he would completely take the reins on "us". To my surprise, *The Secret* turned up the heat, and a string of dates commenced after that first one. I kicked back to enjoy the ride since he was finally putting in effort.

Another Chance

In our new "normal," our lunch and dinner dates were always at restaurants where hardly anyone would frequent. I didn't know then that the restaurants weren't popular because I never knew most of them even existed. They were new experiences for me, so all I was concerned about was trying new dishes. Nothing else was on my mind.

The first official dinner date was at a little restaurant that's tucked away in an apartment complex on the west end of Augusta, quaintly situated right next to the complex's racquet club. The apartment complex and racquet club aren't widely known in the city. I know many who have lived in Augusta all of their lives and have never even heard of the place. Had I not stumbled upon the complex when looking for a place to call home, I would've been among the host of others who had no clue the apartments were there.

Upon arrival at the apartment complex, the restaurant isn't even visible. One would have to know it it's there to know it's there or be on an intentional search to find it, which was the only way I was able to find it the night I met *The Secret* there; he'd given me clear directions, telling me step by step how to navigate to the cove where it was hidden from the rest of the world. It was a cute restaurant, without a doubt, but there was an overly obvious attempt to set an atmosphere for romance that actually detracted from the ambiance. The dimmed lights might as well have been turned off. I could hardly see what was on the table in front of me. The music was low, but it was the kind of low that frustrated music lovers like me. I could hear tunes coming from the speakers that were inconspicuously placed about the dining room, but I couldn't even make out if they were tunes I wanted to sing along with. I was straining my ear to grab hold of any familiar beats or lyrics that would maybe make me more comfortable in that setting and keep my eyes off of the fact that we were only two of four people in the restaurant. When I could see I wouldn't get that comfort, I just tuned the music out altogether.

And then there was the waitress who was literally at our beck and call because there was no one else there for her to serve. That should have been refreshing. It should have been a welcomed luxury not to have to wait to have my drink refilled or have my dinner napkin replaced after the original one hit the floor, but it was irksome. She was never more than a few feet away. It was hard for me to engage in any real conversation when it felt like we were being watched. Being asked, over and over, with hardly enough time to breathe in between, if we were okay or needed anything, was overkill. *The Secret* had nothing to do with what happened once we were inside the restaurant because it was apparent he was about as irritated as I was, but that place and that timing, the Lord showed me, months afterward, that *The Secret* was fully aware of those factors. Taking me to that place at that time was his plan. It was by design that we'd spent the evening in the dark.

Another restaurant *The Secret* took me to was on a side of town where I handled a lot of business. I'd actually passed the place many times and never even noticed it was a restaurant. When we got there, I said, "Oh, this is a restaurant? Who knew?"

When we walked up to the restaurant that chilly fall night with our arms hooked together by our elbows, the hostess was holding the door open for us. She smiled and welcomed us, and as we entered the building, I immediately saw why she'd met us at the door. The restaurant was empty and lifeless. There may have been one or two tables with customers, but the only other souls outside of theirs and *The Secret's* and mine was the restaurant staff. The hosts, waiters, and waitresses were eagerly awaiting customers' arrivals so they'd have some work to do.

Once we were seated and had a chance to look over the menus, our overly excited waitress was at our table to take our orders. Within 10-15 minutes, our food was placed on the table before us, and after about 30 minutes of eating and talking, *The Secret* was paying for our meal and helping me with my jacket so we could head back out into the cool night air. It was a Tuesday evening. A weekday. A school night. Most restaurants see very little traffic then, and *The Secret* knew that. Unbeknownst to me at that time, having dinner there that night was all a part of his plan. I thought he had worked me into his busy schedule.

Then there was the Italian restaurant in downtown Augusta that, at that time, I'd only heard mention of. This dinner date, I remember, was a Sunday night, another one of the slowest nights for any restaurant. Just like the other restaurants, this one was empty. Our waiter, like the waitresses from the other restaurants, was at our beck and call. And the time and place for this date, like all the others, was by design. It was *The Secret's* plan to keep us well hidden behind his curtain.

There were other strategically planned lunches and dinners, but those weren't our only secret outings. We went to the movies once that I remember. When God was showing me, in hindsight, all of the ways *The Secret* was intentionally moving about to keep us in the dark, the one thing I remembered about the movies was how we'd gone to a matinee in the middle of the day when traffic is lightest in the cinema. That day, the theater where our movie was playing was empty. When I thought back on the particulars of that date, I remembered us talking a little in the theater while we waited on the movie to start and the lights were still up. He was slouched down in his seat as he talked about how tired he was from all the work he'd done the couple of days before that movie date. It appeared, then, that he was trying to get comfortable, but it was clear, later, that that slouch had nothing to do with his fatigue. That slouch was deep, and it had purpose. It was a slouch that said, "Even in this empty theater, I need to make sure I'm out of sight."

And I can't even recount the times we met up in random parking lots. It was our way of touching base that became a standard thing for us. If there wasn't enough time after one of his long days for us to really get together, he at least wanted to see me. That was the rationale he gave. If I was out and about when he would call at the end of his work day, we'd just pick a spot somewhere centrally located between where he was and where I was, and we'd meet up. We would park and stand outside of our cars and talk, and sometimes we would sit in one of our cars and talk. One of those times, in particular, maybe two months into "our thing" and before all the official dates, we met up at a CVS. We stood outside of our cars and talked for about 20 minutes. We were erupting with laughter about something he'd shared about an incident at work. When we were coming down off of the laugh, he said he'd better start toward home so he could prepare for an early morning. He was talking through lingering laughter, and I was still pretty tickled myself. He said, "Let's go ahead and wrap this up before somebody sees us," and he chuckled a little more. Still giggling, I said, "Okay," not even realizing that I'd just given him permission for us to continue with the parking lot meet-up foolishness. It wasn't until I got in my car that I realized he'd just said without saying that we were moving about in secret. And although, at that time, so early on, we said we didn't want to say too much about "us" yet, we were still laying a brick on the foundation of whatever it was we were building. That moment set the stage for how we would proceed, and, sure enough, the Bonnie and Clyde meet-ups went on the entire time we were "together". They never stopped. After the fact, and after all was said and done with us, I cringed at the thought of how many times we'd met up that way. How was it that I kept accepting it?

Disobedience

Somewhere in the middle of our widespread secret date-a-thon, I took a moment to assess how things were changing with us as a result of the time we'd been spending together. We had been seeing each other more and talking more, but I still felt like I didn't know him. His quiet, treasure-chest disposition was hard to invade. Our conversations weren't as dead end as they'd once been, but still, it was like pulling teeth getting him to talk about anything concerning us or anything concerning the him that I didn't see with my eyes. He was physically closer, yet still so far away, and I wanted to crack the code. Again, I appreciated the effort he'd put forth in planning more dates for us, so I wanted to match his efforts and plan a date of my own. I wanted to give a little because he was giving a little, and even though I knew the Lord had said I shouldn't entertain company in my home, I thought inviting him into my home, showing him that I was willing to share more of myself with him, would help him relax and know it was okay to share a little more of himself with me. I knew the foods he liked because somewhere in the conversations we'd had over time, I'd learned that. So, I prepared some of his favorites and invited him to my home for lunch.

I hadn't ever cooked for anyone but *The One* and knew I wanted to reserve something so special for someone who deemed me equally as special. That wasn't something I whipped out all willy nilly, but there I was again, just as I'd been with *Rebound*, behaving like I was under a spell. I just went with it. And the whole time while planning the lunch date, I couldn't believe I was going with it. Yes, I had the back and forth conversation with myself about taking such a step. Yes, I doubted. Yes, I called it off a few times within myself, but even while those conversations were going on within me, I kept planning and preparing. I made a hand-written invitation and passed it off to *The Secret* at church, and once that was done, there was no turning back.

I had nervous jitters the day of the lunch as I awaited his arrival. I still couldn't believe, up to the point of *The Secret* ringing my doorbell, that I was actually about to have him in my home. I took a deep breath when I heard the *ding dong* and slowly made my way to the door. Once at the door, I took another deep breath and unlocked and opened it, not realizing I was opening a door to all of me. We greeted with a hug, and he handed me a gift. I thanked him for his thoughtfulness and welcomed him in, showing him to the adjoining kitchen and dining room. He grabbed a seat on one of the bar stools at the counter and watched me move about the kitchen as I took care of last-minute things. He smiled and sniffed and said, "It smells good in here." I took pride in knowing the visit was already off to a pleasant start for him.

While we ate, I could tell he was relaxed because he smiled a silly school-boy smile the whole time. The ease in his posture gave it away too. We shared a few laughs over the meal, and he thanked me for cooking the foods he liked. It was evident he wanted to sit at that counter and talk more, and if I didn't have plans for something later that day, we probably would have sat and talked into the evening. I knew I'd broken down one of his walls and that he understood my gesture as an attempt to initiate something more with us. I was grateful and hopeful for what would possibly come later, but that moment, as good as it was, was a catch-22.

As I said, when I opened the door to my home that day, I opened the door to all of me. I had officially let *The Secret* into my most intimate and personal space, not realizing that having him in my home would expose me to a subtle, but very present vulnerability. But God knew, and that was the very thing He had wanted to shield me from. When He told me not to invite suitors into my home, there was a reason for it, even if I couldn't see or understand the reason. God knew the place where I relaxed and let down my hair was reserved for relationships of mutual trust and respect. He knew everyone wasn't supposed to "know me" in my home. God knew *The Secret* wouldn't respect the depth of all that was connected to me sharing my living space with him. It was too big a gesture for him and the triviality of our "relationship". He would be grateful to have been invited, no doubt. He would even be respectful of the home itself, but the introspection and spiritual insight it takes to value what it means for someone to share their sacred space, he wouldn't be able to honor because he didn't honor me.

Nonetheless, he was able to interpret the surface-level revelation from it all, and he knew that opening my home said, without saying, that I trusted him. He interpreted it just as God knew he would. Even if I didn't trust him, and I most certainly did not, the damage was done. Now he "knew me" in a new way. A silent exchange had taken place. Even with my not trusting him, having him in my home connected us in a way that would make me want to share more with him, and I didn't even know it. I couldn't see that I would be more willing to open up in other areas because I'd already invited him into an area that not everyone else had access to. Our connecting in my home had become a secret to be enjoyed between just us, and if we had more secrets to share from then on, they would just be added to the wall of secrets we'd already built together. It would all be just ours, and for someone whose sole plan was to keep us a secret, he would really be able to dig his heels in and work whatever behind-the-curtain magic he wanted to. I wouldn't even have to give consent. I'd already done that when I opened my door.

After the lunch date in my home, I allowed *The Secret* even deeper into my personal space. It was inevitable. We were talking on the phone one night, and he asked, "Why don't you ever kiss me?" I vividly recall choosing not to answer the question truthfully. Instead, I shrugged it off with an "I don't know" because when I heard the question, I had to tune into my thoughts to process it. All I could do was come up with my own question in response to his. I was thinking, *Why would I kiss you?* I couldn't believe he'd even asked! I didn't think *The Secret* was worthy of a kiss from me. I *knew* he wasn't. People who share kisses are committed to each other, and we definitely weren't. I didn't even know what we were calling "us" or if there even *was* an "us," so the thought of kissing him never even crossed my mind.

After that phone call, we had a couple of dinner dates and a few after-work meet-ups in random parking lots. One of those days, I was out and about and *The Secret* called me. While on the call, we realized we were on the same side of town, so he asked me to stop and meet him in a strip mall parking lot. As was our routine, we stepped outside of our vehicles to chat. We talked for a few minutes about the happenings of our day and about what our schedules looked like for the remainder of the week. Then, when we'd said all we needed to say, he walked me to the driver's side of my car. He said his parting words, letting me know he'd call me later. I replied with "Okay" and then we hugged our usual hug. I held on a little longer than normal to build up my nerve because I knew when we pulled away from the embrace, I would be kissing him. When I felt I had enough gall, I pulled away, looked him right in his eyes, leaned in, and kissed him. It went on for what seemed like forever because I knew, no matter how I tried to convince myself otherwise, I was, in fact, kissing a stranger.

As much as I hate to admit it, I kissed *The Secret* just to appease him. I was going through the motions. For weeks, his question had been swarming around in my mind, and although he hadn't said anything about it but that one time, I felt like he was thinking about it every time we were together. I felt like he was waiting around to see what I would do. I wanted to stop the quiet nagging in the back of my mind, so I just went for it. Looking back, it's almost as if I was going through a period where I'd completely taken off the woman of God I'd become and traded it for the likeness of a puppet.

Then, there was the weird out-of-body experience that overtook me when I kissed him. I literally felt a piece of me, a fraction of my spirit, escape my body in that exchange. It was as if I'd given myself away. When I stepped back from the kiss, I felt a moment of emptiness, a hollowing in the pit of my stomach. A sadness overwhelmed me as I hurriedly plopped onto the driver's seat of my car. I wanted to take my kiss back. I closed my door and sat there for a moment, dazed, wondering what I'd just done and why I'd done it. Right then, I realized that even in sharing a kiss, I was giving a piece of myself away. It was more spiritual than anything. I felt the Lord telling me, *"Iantha, this is why physical intimacy should be reserved for your husband inside a relationship where the two of you have decided, without physical intimacy, that you're committed to one another. The physical intimacy, then, will be the icing on the cake. In that relationship, you won't know this emptiness. You'll be fulfilled."*

We kissed a few more times in the weeks that followed, but it wasn't long before I was keeping my kisses to myself. The Lord had been playing that message on repeat in my heart... *"In your marriage relationship, you won't know this emptiness. You'll be fulfilled."* I determined, then, in 2006, that I wouldn't be kissing another man until I kissed my husband at the altar.

Uncovering the Secret

We were eight or nine months into "our thing," and I still hadn't introduced *The Secret* to anyone. It wasn't that I didn't want to. I honestly didn't even know how. I always had a knowing within me that he just wanted to stay hidden, so I let him remain behind the curtain, which meant, inevitably, that I was behind the curtain with him. I remember trying to explain my "relationship" with *The Secret* to a couple of my closest Louisiana friends. Although I would feel like my explanations made it seem as if *The Secret* was all about me and our "relationship," I knew my friends could see through it, and I knew they knew that I knew they could see through it.

Right around this time, my best friend and accountability partner visited me in Augusta for a week. She had heard me talk about *The Secret*, and I'd painted a picture of him that I was sure she wanted to see for herself, but I had nothing to show. I knew she would see that *The Secret* wasn't God's best for me, and I knew she would question my being with him because I knew nothing about him beyond where he worked and where he went to church. I didn't even want to put myself under her microscope.

I hated conjuring up explanations about *The Secret's* absence while she was visiting, but I knew I had to. I talked around the questions she asked. I made sure our schedule had very little down time so there would be no time for her to meet him. I talked in code and excused myself from her presence whenever *The Secret* called. It was a mess, and it was so unlike me. It was obvious that all of my explaining and covering up and uncomfortable inability to speak confidently was my way of saying, *There's really nothing there. We are nothing. We have nothing.* I was embarrassed and so deeply ashamed because my best friend and I shared everything; there were no secrets between us until *The Secret.*

And that's what did it for me.

It took my best friend stepping inside my world for me to see that I'd isolated myself into a danger zone that survived on secrecy, and I knew that danger zone wasn't where I wanted to be. Something on the inside of me finally accepted the message that had been plainly written before me from the very beginning. I told myself that what *The Secret* and I had was going nowhere. I just went ahead and called it what it was. The hope that I had for the possibility of an "us" was an empty one. I'd been played all that time, and that was just that. And with that realization, things got real ugly. I had never been anyone's secret, and I wasn't about to *knowingly* be one.

It was a Sunday afternoon. *The Secret* had taken a trip to Atlanta. All that day, and all the night before when I'd had the epiphany, I rehearsed everything in my mind that had happened with us up to that point. I thought about the things God had shown me about *The Secret's* "behind the curtain" behaviors. I thought about how unfulfilled I felt. I thought about how much I didn't know about *The Secret* and how I'd shared so much of me and he'd shared hardly anything. I thought about how I didn't even know where he lived and how I barely heard mention of anyone in his life. I recognized how pointless my time with him had been, and I realized I was mad at him because he knew he was stringing me along. I was even more upset with myself for allowing it to happen. He began to be the craving. I could see him and I could reach and almost touch him, but I never did. I had been hanging on by a thread in search of commitment from him, but how I'd allowed myself to go about getting it was not God's design. I had disobeyed the Lord, and I was surely suffering the consequences.

I decided to give *The Secret* a call when I knew he'd be on the road headed back to Augusta. I was so angry when I picked up the phone to call him that I could see my hands shaking. When I got him on the phone, our conversation started normally with annoying, unnecessary pleasantries, and it progressed as it always did with unfulfilling, meaningless small talk. I let that go on for a couple of minutes, but then, I unleashed my rage. I was a dam whose walls had burst, and it was well beyond time for the waters to flow. I let him have it! I don't remember any of what I said in that frustrated rant, but I have a crystal clear memory of what I was feeling.

I couldn't believe he didn't honor me and was intentionally tucking me away in the dark. I felt so violated. I felt used. I felt like the dumb girl. My pride was torched. The "Lady I" who wouldn't dare allow a man to give her anything but the royal treatment had fallen into a trap. My insides were scarred and they were tender to the touch. I. Was. Mad! And although we never physically exchanged anything but kisses, God showed me my emotions and my spirit were connected to those kisses. I couldn't take them back. And that hurt.

I yelled at him, and I didn't stop yelling until I said all I felt I needed to say. He got a few words in, but not many. I didn't let him. I'd been asking questions and trying to figure us out for months, to no avail. He'd had his time to talk. It was my turn. Eventually, of course, dealing with the matter at hand was too much for him, so he found a way to end the conversation, and that was fine by me. By that time, I'd said what I needed to say.

Later that night, we continued with an hour or so of heated texting. I still didn't understand why he was holding back. I had never been in a position like that, to feel like I wasn't worthy of someone's time. And there were still no answers. *The Secret* even wanted to talk and text like nothing had ever happened, as if there wasn't still a huge abyss of undealt with mess between us. But I wasn't allowing him to ignore me anymore. I was determined to be heard.

Since he avoided real conversations at all costs and ran from talking about what was right before us, I decided to write a letter. It was a shame that I had to talk to him in a letter, but again, I wasn't about to be silenced. I'd walked through almost a full year of his foolishness, and I was going to say what I needed to say before I completely removed myself from his invisible grip. I wasn't carrying anything with me when I left. After a few weeks of silence between us and much prayer, I had completely sorted through my feelings and settled on what I wanted to say. It came out like this…

If you've opened this, and you don't have adequate time to really sit down and read, you may want to close it and pick it back up when you have the time. I just have to tell you how I feel. I won't be completely free until I do. I've never really been able to tell you how certain things have affected me, and although I've forgiven you and do not hold anything against you, I still need to release. You have to know.

I've thought and thought and thought some more of how to say everything I want to say. It's quite a bit, so things get jumbled up in my head. The easiest way, I found, was for me to write it all out. Things always come out better for me that way. Plus, to be frankly honest, I'm tired of talking. That doesn't seem to do much in this case. Lastly, this way is a little less threatening, and since talking seems to make you feel attacked, I opted to make you comfortable…again.

In this letter, I'm sure I'll be asking a lot of questions because I have about a million of them running through my head.

So…here goes…

The Secret, I gave you another chance against everything within me that was screaming NO. I was angry, and naturally, I didn't want to have anything to do with you. Because I care about you, though, and the potential we had, I wanted to give you the opportunity to try again to do whatever it is you felt like you needed to do. I turned the tables and asked myself if I would want that same chance in a situation like ours. I know, without a doubt, that the Lord was teaching me what HIS forgiveness looks like. He used our situation to show me how many chances He gives us and how we don't always get it right, yet he pardons us. My mistake, however, was thinking that forgiving you meant I had to be with you. I thought that if I was forgiving you, I should just go ahead on and start the clean slate, but all I needed to do was just forgive, let you know that I had forgiven you, and move on. I certainly wish I would've done that because...

I hate this relationship, or whatever it is that we've had, and had I let it go with the forgiveness I issued then, I'd probably be in the clear right now. It's been nothing but confusing, misleading, unfulfilling and rollercoastery for the most part. That is the LAST thing I need in my life. **Is my peace destroyed at this point?** Most definitely! And this is not what I signed up for—it's not what I want. I don't deserve you, and you don't deserve me. I keep expecting you to be someone that you're not, and to do things that **SHOW** you actually want this thing to go somewhere, and it's been a little too much work for me— more than I want to put in for the return it's been getting. The things I want to offer, you're not ready to handle with the proper respect and level of reciprocation that they require. I feel like I've wasted my time, and I won't do that anymore.

Here's where all of this comes from...

You say one thing, and do something else. I don't operate like that, so it's very hard for me to accept. From jump, we established that we don't do aimless dating. I was sizing you up and you were sizing me up to see if we were "long haul" potential. When I'm considering someone to be "long haul," a spiritual leader and protector, that's one of the first things I look for—someone to say it and do it. I don't believe that that quality is not present within you. I just haven't seen it consistently over a year's time, and that, frankly, is enough for me. That, to me, says that's who you are. I can't change that. You have to, and it doesn't seem like, at this point, you're ready to.

It's simple things like saying you're going to call back. That means a lot. It just says you keep your word. It's not about the call, believe me, because I would rather not even talk on the phone, but it's about me being important enough for you to even remember that you said you'd call me back. (Things that aren't important to us slip our minds.) I'm still waiting on your mother to get back from church, and I'm still waiting on your aunt to call you so she can let you know she's going to release you from your caretaking responsibility with your cousin.

You've been trying so hard to win me that you've lost me. I've told you that I don't throw out idle words, and I hate when people do it. There's so much power in the tongue that we can't dare say everything we think. When you carelessly use words to flatter and appease me, it does nothing, really, but worsen the situation. For instance, I think that marriage talk would most definitely be flattering to most women who've never been married, but since I'm not in a rush to the altar, I could hear you say you want to marry me, and talk about a ring, and a car for the family and all the other things you've thrown out, and it'll go in one ear and out the other. It's fun to entertain every once in a while to make conversation, but when we look long, hard, and deep at this thing, come on.

I know, for a fact, *The Secret*, that if I were to seriously address the marriage issue, you'd run and hide, and avoid, and push it as far away as possible because you're not ready to deal with it—and I KNOW you're not. You can't even define this relationship, so I know marriage is out of the question. When you do that—play around with the words you say, thinking that that will make a heavy situation light (because you do it mostly in times of disagreement or unnecessary confusion)—it only does the exact opposite. It adds fuel to the fire because I know how much you're doing it just to "sound good".

And here comes the "I'm in love with you" statement. Do I believe that you feel that strongly? I do. But because IT DOES NOT SHOW UP, it voids your feeling out. I told you once before, you can tell me all day long that you love me, but until I see it, I don't believe it. I've shown my love for you, *The Secret*, because my love for you causes me to do so. I've NEVER known one to work apart from the other because they don't. Your talk has been pointless.

"I was trying, but I just didn't have time." How in the world don't you have time for something or someone who's important to you? Explain that one to me. Even if you feel like you don't have time, you don't say it! And you CONSTANTLY say it! And it's been CONSTANTLY building a fortified wall within me. I'm tired of bringing that to your attention only for it to not be dealt with. And the statement has been, and will always be true—you make time for what's important in your life. If your life was filled with too much, doggone it, you knew it when you asked me into it. You don't ask someone to dinner and eat at another table! Saying you don't have time is probably the highest insult you've ever paid me, and after so many times…

I can't believe you'd even tell me you care like you do and not have it show up in the time you give to me/us. That is really beyond me. There have been times that I've sacrificed my time to do a lot of other VERY important things because I WANTED to be with you to foster the relationship that I thought we both wanted. I knew those things would be there, right where I left them, and I planned accordingly to be able to get to them and do what needed to be done. I can't say that I've seen the same thing from you.

I've concluded that you really don't have the time, and you just don't want to admit to that. Instead, you drag this thing on and on. Stepping out of the relationship is a lot better than saying, "I do have time, but…" Just call it what it is. You aren't able to do the relationship thing right now. I would've had a great deal of respect for you admitting to that—much more than being dragged around like I have been because you want to hold on for safe keeping and for "one day, someday". And I only hope you won't enter another relationship/situation without taking care of you first. That is my prayer, because my heart hurts every time I think about this possibly happening to someone else. Oh my God!

Sadly, at some point, it got to where I didn't even want to ask you to do things, and I didn't, because I was so sure I would hear that you "didn't have time". How can a relationship even work like that? I'm so wounded that I can't even build up enough guns to ask the one, who's supposed to be that one, to spend time with me. That's crazy! And it's also pointless, which leads me to…

I'm constantly asking myself lately, "Why is he even here?" I do everything by myself anyway, so what do I need him for?

I've never seen a man who's in love with a woman show so little concern for what's important in her life. When I mentioned I was going to New York, you said nothing. When I mentioned it again, you said nothing. When I texted it, you said nothing. And when I mentioned it again, you said nothing. Nothing at all! Wow! I have never felt so…I don't even know the word I want.

I've never known a man to be <u>in love with</u> a woman, yet keep her from people and things that are important to him. You're so protective, and that, too, has been pretty doggone offensive. That has to be the second highest insult you've paid me. I believe there's something in you that never even expected this to work, and because of that, you didn't let me get too close so when you did mess up, you wouldn't have to undo anything or clean up any mess. I would've never allowed anything to harm you in any way, *The Secret*, if it was in my power to avoid it. What's precious to you would've been just as precious to me. All I've ever been is there for you because that's genuinely where I wanted to be, and not being able to share even the littlest things with you like your home, for instance, is heartbreaking. I opened my home to you and shared one of the things that's closest to me because I was willing to sacrifice for something we both said we wanted. Your best friend, the person you're with five days or more out of the week, doesn't even know me. I would've loved to offer my condolences to his family, but I had to sit by and watch because the one who's **in love with** me never mentioned that I was as much a part of his life as I was.

I've given, given, given, and you've taken, taken, taken. Never in my life have I felt so used and unappreciated and violated, and, yes, even disrespected. I thank God that my worth is measured in His sight and not man's because if it were not, I'd be one depressed sister. I'm hurt, no doubt, but I think you'll be more hurt when you look up one day and realize just how much I was willing to give to you, do for you, and be to/for you. I don't deserve you, *The Secret*, and you don't deserve me.

So let's just call it what it is.

Did the letter shock you too? Until I pulled it from an old computer to use in this chapter, I had completely forgotten that *The Secret* would sometimes tell me he loved me and that he was in love with me. I actually laughed when I read the letter for the first time after deciding to include it in the book. I just *could not* believe it! And had we really talked in the beginning of "our thing" about considering each other for the long haul? *Really?* I laughed some more after trying to wrap my mind around that. I guess because I knew there was never any depth or real truth to marriage talk with us, I never even counted it as real in my mind. He was a charmer, and I'll talk more about that when we get to the "Spotlight on the Secret" section. In the end, I guess all I could see was the summation of the foolishness that "our thing" was. I remembered what stuck with me the most, and that was—I was a secret. We were behind the curtain, in the dark, and that never felt like love. And it certainly didn't say marriage. Reading that letter was almost like looking at myself in a picture from my childhood. You know how it is when you see yourself and can't believe you wore that dress or that your mom combed your hair that way or, goodness, that you even liked those shoes? It was that kind of feeling. I had to read it several times to remind myself that I was, in fact, the one who wrote the letter. It was like, *Yes, Iantha. This was you. This is your truth.*

I went back as far as I could in my mind to try to remember instances when he said those things, but I came up with nothing. I just *could not* remember, and in that moment, I thanked God! It's amazing how the Lord can free us of memories that we don't need.

My Turn Now

After I passed that four-page typed letter off to *The Secret* at church, I was done. I never wanted to experience anything quite like I experienced with him again. So, to protect myself from him and everything that reminded me of him and what I'd been put through, I became my own personal firewall, and nothing connected to him was getting past that wall into my heart. I was a ball of anger on the inside, a raging storm of emotion when it came to him. That meant I was short with him whenever I saw him, and in most cases, I wouldn't speak at all. Craftily excluding him with not even a second thought or ignoring him altogether was my way of coping with the hurt. I was guarded and defensive; I was ashamed that I'd let myself become his secret.

And, oh, how the tables turned after he received my letter! All of a sudden, he would speak all the time, no matter where we were. He would even try to stop me to talk if I was walking by him at church, which did nothing but infuriate me even more. I would make it my business to walk right past him and not even look his way. In my eyes, he wasn't even there. My thoughts were, *Didn't you wanna treat me like I didn't exist? Well, here ya go, homeboy. Let's not switch things up. Let's keep that same energy.*

There would be moments at church when I would see him looking at me from across the room. I would purposely make eye contact with him and hold it for a few seconds just so I could roll my eyes and intentionally redirect my attention elsewhere. There would be the usual clusters of conversations going on after church in the vestibule. *The Secret*, remember, wouldn't normally join any discussions that were already in progress, but surprisingly he was interested in being a part of the conversations I was having with others. I would talk to everybody in the group but him. I remember a specific instance pretty clearly. *The Secret* interjected a statement in response to what one of the brothers in our circle had said. Everyone nodded their heads in agreement with his addition to the conversation, but I looked at our brother who'd made the original comment and said, "Okay. So, anyway. What were you saying?"

Not long after I gave *The Secret* the letter, there was a wedding for a couple that attended his church. We both attended the wedding. He found me at the reception and sat at the table where I was seated with a couple of my mentees and other children from my church. He was trying his best to talk to me, but I wasn't having it. He told me, as he talked to the side of my very obviously uninterested face, that the letter really hurt him because it caused him to have to look at who he really was. He was being sincere, but I trampled all over the sincerity in whatever words he spoke that night. Every now and then between his words, I would glare at him with the hate a mother has for her child's abuser. Then, I would hold that glare for a bit and then coldly turn my eyes back off into the distance from whence they came. Once or twice, I looked at him, shook my head, and sniggled with disdain. He tried to grab my hand and you would've thought he was trying to murder me. I pulled my hand away from him with such force that he had to take a little scoot back in his seat. I served that yanking of my hand with a glint of death that said, *Don't you dare touch me. You don't deserve the privilege of being that close to me.* And you know what? Now that I think about it, I think I actually said something like that to him. Honey, he had done what no man had ever done before, and I was angry! As I told him in the letter, had I not known my worth, he could have completely destroyed my self-esteem. And I think he knew it. But to his surprise, I brought his schemes and charm to a screeching halt.

For weeks after that wedding, there were daily texts from him. Most of them got no response from me. The few I *did* respond to, I'm sure were harsh. I let him know how being mistreated felt. But eventually, the Lord grabbed hold of my heart and had me to take a long, hard look at myself. He reminded me of what I'd learned from my time with *Rebound*. I needed to run to the Lord with my hurt, so I went on a fast to take my heart and all its concerns to the Lord. I needed to cry. I needed to vent. I needed to ask God to help me get past the shame and embarrassment I felt. I needed to repent for having disobeyed the Lord. I needed His comfort, and I needed to regain my peace. For three days, I drank only water, and I prayed and sought the Lord. I laid everything out before Him.

God's Turn

I was in prayer on the last morning of my fast, and the Lord told me to prepare a breakfast for *The Secret* and take it to his job. Now, upon first hearing it, naturally, I thought I'd heard wrong. God certainly wasn't telling me to prepare a meal, the ultimate act of love, for that man. And not only prepare the meal, but take it to his job. Naw. I hadn't heard that. There was no way. But years prior, I had learned something in my walk with the Lord about knowing for sure if I'm hearing Him speak. I learned that God will never tell me to do anything that will hurt or harm anyone. To be a blessing to someone, especially when I don't want to be, is an indication that I'm hearing from God. That's definitely not the enemy. Making *The Secret* breakfast or doing anything kind for him was not on my agenda, so it HAD TO BE God.

I had seen the results of not doing what God clearly said do, and the pain of the consequences was still a little too fresh, so once I got past my feelings and settled it within myself that the Lord had given me very clear instructions, I not only prepared that breakfast, but I found myself, after a little more prayer, joyfully preparing it. In the midst of the preparation, I began praying for *The Secret*. The Holy Spirit had me praying things that only His wisdom could have had me pray because I did not want to pray for that man. I didn't even have the words to pray for him. I hated that the Lord chose as grand a gesture as breakfast because I knew what *The Secret* would think. He would think I wanted to reconnect with him.

I didn't even let *The Secret* know breakfast was coming. I just texted him when I was outside of his workplace and told him to come out and get something I had for him. Confusion was all over his face when he met me at my car. I gave him a hug and handed him his hot breakfast. His confusion instantly shifted to shock. He asked, "What is this?" I had to explain to him that that's what the Lord told me to do.

I said, "I was awful toward you. Yes, you hurt me with the way you treated me, but it doesn't give me the right to mistreat you."

That was what God had shown me during the fast. He showed me my heart. He showed me that I was ungodly in my vengeance toward *The Secret*. I wasn't kind and I hadn't truly forgiven him. I didn't offer any grace, and when *The Secret* tried to talk to me about how I had actually helped him to see the error of his ways, I ignored him. The Lord had me to prepare breakfast for *The Secret* to show him GOD's love. He wanted *The Secret* to see that He had forgiven him, and God wanted me to see that if He could forgive him, I had a responsibility to forgive him too. The breakfast was a start.

Just like I knew would happen, *The Secret* thought breakfast was an open door for him to try to weasel his way back into conversation with me. He thanked me by text, and I responded to that one text by reiterating my apologies for having treated him the way I had. He wanted to continue texting after that, but I didn't respond. He even called a time or two. I ignored the calls too. I'd done what God had told me to do, and I needed some time alone with no distractions to allow God to completely heal my heart.

In the months that followed, I walked through some situations in other relationships where I got to see what it felt like to have godly sorrow for having wronged someone and what it felt like to need their forgiveness. One such situation was with a church sister, *The Lesson*.

The Lesson and I were working on a month-long church project together, and everything was going well with our planning and preparation until our lines of communication got crossed.

In our partnership, *The Lesson* took the lead on handling the logistics for the project and for securing outside vendors for supplies we needed. That's where she was strong. I was responsible for scheduling and assisting with logistics, but my biggest responsibility was balancing the project budget and writing checks. Because of how I plan and process, I had a day set aside, once a week, when I would manage all of our transactions and write any necessary checks. I never explained my process to *The Lesson* because there was never a need; when we needed checks, they were always ready. One time, though, *The Lesson* needed a check for a particular vendor, and she needed it on the spot.

On the day she asked for the check, I hadn't written any checks for that week. I was planning to write the checks in a couple of days because I had some balancing to do once a few transactions were processed. I wanted to balance all at once when I had the opportunity to lay everything out and see the big picture. *The Lesson* wanted to pay that vendor right then. I couldn't understand what the rush was all about because there wasn't a set due date for that vendor in our payment schedule. I told her I would be writing the check in a couple days and I would get it to her. I thought we were having a regular conversation like we'd always had about the budget, but my saying that I wouldn't be writing checks for a couple days set our relationship ablaze!

What I didn't know was that *The Lesson* had a long-standing working relationship with that vendor and she didn't want to ruin it. She thought surely that not paying them that day would ruin everything, but she didn't explain that to me. She just kept saying she needed the check because she was going to be on that side of town and wanted to go ahead and make payment. I was thinking she would understand that I just wanted to balance the budget so I didn't mess anything up, but I didn't explain that to her. It was a classic case of miscommunication. When I gave *The Lesson* that check a couple days later so she could get it to the vendor, she let me know, with a snatch of the check, a roll of her eyes, and a fierce silence that she and I were not okay.

After that day, and for quite some time, *The Lesson* was angry with me. She hurled hurt my way every chance she got, and she even did it through other people. She accused me of being involved in gossip about her. If there was someone that I was in close relationship with at church, she stopped talking to them as she normally would simply because I was connected to them. She completely shut herself off from me and would make it her business to let me know she had. I tried so many times to talk to her like we normally would, but she would shut me down. I would speak to her or try to talk to her in one of the clusters after church, and she would straight up ignore me. I cried so much in that season because no matter what I tried, she wasn't having it.

Months later, I went to her in tears. I said, "Whatever I've done to you, however I've hurt you, I am *so* sorry." And she embraced me. I didn't know then that not writing the check that day was the onset of both of our pain. I later learned that she was hurt because it seemed as if I didn't care how she felt about the business relationship she'd worked so hard to establish. I never knew that was how she felt. I'd hurt her and she made me pay, just like I had been making *The Secret* pay. God took me right back to *The Secret* and me and showed me how it felt to be on the receiving end. He showed me how it felt to express godly sorrow for a wound I inflicted. I wanted *The Lesson* to know, from the depths of my being, that I needed her forgiveness. I didn't want our relationship to be in shambles anymore. I hurt so badly knowing I'd hurt her, and God showed me that *The Secret* hurt pretty badly too when he learned he'd hurt me. *The Secret* knew he had done wrong by me, but the words of my letter sobered him and made him take a look at himself. He really was sorry for bringing me so much pain, and he wanted to offer me a genuine apology, but I shut him out just like *The Lesson* had done me. So, after *The Lesson* and I apologized to each other and our relationship was restored, I knew I had to contact *The Secret* and ask for his forgiveness for so coldly disregarding him and not allowing him the floor to make reparations. There was no question about it.

The Secret was playing tough when I first reached out to him, and he didn't want to hear from me right then, but eventually, he allowed me to apologize, and I, for the first time, received an apology from him. And just as his track record had proven, when that door opened again after months and months of no communication, he tried to walk right in. I laughed when I ignored all his texts and phone calls that followed. I just thought to myself, *Some things never change. Is he really trying to pull me behind the curtain and hide me again?*

It was a sure sign—not that I needed another one—that...

He wasn't it either.

Spotlight on
The Secret

If it has to be done in the dark,
honey, ain't no light in it.

Spotlight on The Secret #1 – There's a certain level of privacy and exclusivity that everyone wants in their relationships, but the relationship itself shouldn't be a secret.

There are secrets that we sometimes keep to maybe surprise friends or loved ones, and there are instances when we withhold exciting news for an appropriate and expected reveal. Those secrets always have an expiration date with the intention of being unveiled for the enjoyment of all parties involved. Then, there are secrets that dictionary.com defines as "mysteries designed to escape notice, knowledge, or observation." Those secrets don't necessarily have an expiration date. In fact, in most cases, the intent is for those secrets to always be secrets. The intent is for them to forever remain in the dark, and your relationship shouldn't be that kind of secret.

If only the two of you know about the two of you, you're in the dark, and that's a problem. If people in your close circle know about you and your "secret," but can't share with even "the secret" that they know about the relationship, you're in the dark, and that's a problem. If a couple of his boys know about the two of you, but they can't even share with you that they know, or they only share in hushes that they're aware of the two of you, you're in the dark, and that's a problem. A relationship that operates only in the dark is unhealthy, and it's a train wreck waiting to happen. You shouldn't have to talk in hushes about your relationship. You shouldn't have to hide that you two talk and hang out on a regular basis. You shouldn't have to wonder if you should introduce him to anyone, or if he'll be okay being introduced to the people in your life—and all of the other "you shouldn't" scenarios I shared in my telling of the time I spent with *The Secret*.

I'll never forget my pastor saying, "Yeah, Sister I. Whenever you meet whoever you think you wanna date, bring him on over here. Let us (pastor and his wife) meet him and get to know him because, see, we don't love him as good as you do. We can see what you ain't gon' see in the love cloud." And it's true. It's true in any relationship. People outside of the relationship can see things that the two of you won't see when you're locked up in each other's eyes. We all need the people in our lives to know about our relationships. It's for our good. We need accountability, wise counsel, encouragement, and warnings, and that doesn't happen if we're in the dark where no one can see us.

Spotlight on The Secret #2 – When he's avoiding the conversation to define the relationship, there is no relationship, and he doesn't want one.

The Secret is where I learned that if a man says (shows) he doesn't want something, he really doesn't want it. *The Secret* never *said* he didn't want to be with me, but he certainly *showed* it, which was just like saying it. It was the first time in my life that a man had ever shown me anything along the lines of not wanting to be with me completely and exclusively, and, honestly, my pride was having a hard time accepting it. Why would he *not* want to be with me as completely and exclusively as everyone else had?

For some time, I put more hopeful expectation in what *The Secret* was saying instead of weighing what he was *doing*. Mistake. And it's one I don't want you to make.

If he's talking like he's all in, but he's not walking like it, he doesn't want the relationship. If he's not willing to talk about his intentions for you and the relationship and can't articulate where he sees the two of you going as a couple, he doesn't want the relationship. Now, if both of you are avoiding the conversation about where you stand as a couple because you agree it's too soon or there's some other circumstance, that's understandable. There's usually a time constraint for that, and again, it's mutual. But when one of you is constantly running from the conversation about the state of the relationship, that's a problem and a sign that that one doesn't want the relationship. How can the two of you be together if you can't agree on even being together?

I Corinthians 14:33 KJV says, "God is not the author of confusion, but of peace…" It's clear when God agrees with a thing because His stamp of approval is His peace. If there's confusion—you constantly questioning what's going on with the relationship—how can you also have peace—an absolute knowing that all is well? And if you're His and everything in your life is to be a reflection of Him, why would you want to be in a relationship that doesn't have His peace?

I want to share this thought from something I saw floating around social media. It says, "Life is too short for me to wait on you to figure out if you want to be with me." How true it is! If he doesn't want the relationship, it's okay. Be grateful that you were able to see it. Make the decision of quality to leave. Don't allow him to waste your time.

Spotlight on the Secret #3 – If most of your dates and meet ups are on one person's time, you're not in a relationship, and there are secrets.

As much as I didn't want to believe or admit it, I had to finally come to terms with the truth—*The Secret* had secrets *(that I still don't know about to this day)*. I had to tell myself:

- If he is this closed and this consistent with seeing me only on certain days of the week, he has secrets.
- If we can never really talk about "what" we are or that we're having as much contact outside of church as we are, he has secrets.
- It was sweet and kind of romantic at first, but if *everywhere* we go is his choice, he has secrets *(or control issues, and that's whole 'notha book)*.

- If I suggest a time and place for something I want to do, and it eventually gets craftily scheduled around his time, he has secrets.

Again, relationships are open. Both people in the relationship should have a say in when you do things and where you go, and there's a willing compromise on both ends. Sometimes one person's schedule has to do some twisting, and sometimes the other's does. There's even the possibility that both schedules will have to be tweaked. Never should there ever be a time when the relationship is only what one person says. That's not a relationship. That's a dictatorship. And it's deceitful and dark. And there are secrets. And that's all I have to say about that.

Spotlight on The Secret #4 – Don't compromise your convictions. You'll regret it every time.

When the Lord places convictions in our hearts or gives us direct instruction on what or what not to do, it's for our good. God may not tell us exactly *why* we need to do a thing, but it doesn't matter. It's our duty to just trust that His reasoning is for our good and to simply obey. The Lord directs us and gives us instruction because he already knows what's ahead. He orchestrates our end from our beginning. He orders our steps because He knows all things.

God gave me two clear directives: (1) "Don't initiate anything with any man." I did it anyway, even though it was *completely* out of my character, and I regretted it. (2) "Don't invite any suitors into my home." I did it anyway, and I regretted it.

Disobedience is the breeding ground for disaster, and I'm a living witness. The moment I took my eyes off of how the Lord told me to handle myself in relationships, the jaws of the trap shut down on me and gripped tightly. I incurred unnecessary pain as a result of my disobedience, and now you have read a whole chapter about it. Lessons were learned, for sure, but they came from situations I shouldn't have even had to walk through. I brought those on myself when I disregarded the Lord's protection that came through his directives. He knew what would come of it, and because He loves me, He wanted me to avoid the pitfalls. He wants the same for you.

When we walk away from God's safety, we toss away his covering. When we disobey, we thrust ourselves out to the wolves, so we shouldn't be surprised when we feel attacks. Some lessons we don't even have to learn. Some classes we don't even have to take. Don't just hear what God says. Do what He says. It's for your good.

Spotlight on The Secret #5 – Let a sleeping dog lie. If it wants to play, it'll come running.

I am not implying anything derogatory here. I don't think *The Secret* or any other man is a dog. I actually don't like the saying that men are dogs. What this figurative statement is saying, though, is if a man wants a woman, he will pursue her because when men know what they want, they don't stop short of getting it.

If he comes to find you, he's probably ready to lead and has a clear mission in sight for a relationship. If he doesn't, and you went to him and sought him out, you'll never even know if he was ready with a mission in sight for a relationship. Men don't mind women letting them know they're interested in them because men want to know they're desired too, but a man, generally, wants to be the one initiating "the chase". Women don't have to pursue. If a man wants a woman, he "comes running".

Is this always the case? Of course not. There are no absolutes. But know this, woman: If he's not ready, he's not ready. Don't try to make him ready. That will end in more frustration for you than it will for him. If you see he's not running in your direction, "let him sleep."

Spotlight on The Secret #6 – Beware of the charmer.

One day, the Lord spoke the following words to my spirit and told me to post them on social media: Ladies, beware of charmers. They're full of words, but they don't want anything beyond your blushes from their compliments. They seek attention and praise for *being* "gentlemen". They pour on pointless flattery just to hear themselves talk and to "look good" in your eyes. There is no destination or end goal in sight. The only mission is to charm you around and around in a circle. Don't allow yourself to get dizzy.

I could write this only because I've been there. Beware of the charmer.

Spotlight on The Secret Final Thoughts

- You won't have to ask him to define the relationship. He'll do that without your prompting.
- You won't have to be hidden and out of sight because he will want to show you off.
- You won't have to speak in hushes or wonder if you should mention "your relationship" at all. He'll be shouting it from the rooftops.
- He will make sacrifices to be clear about where the relationship stands. He'll make himself uncomfortable to be clear. And he'll be clear with any and everybody, not just you.
- A man goes after what he wants. He refuses to let anyone else have it if he knows he's found his prize. He protects it and takes every measure to make sure it doesn't get away.
- A man who is serious thinks *marriage* because he knows that's the finality of gaining you for himself.
- Men who don't want you make excuses. They hide. They drag you around to try to figure out what they want to do. They even look elsewhere to make sure they're not missing

out before they make that last move to close the deal on you. They're not serious. They don't know what they want.

- If he's not showing you in more ways than one that he's serious about being with you, he's not.

Tweet your takeaways from *The Secret*.
#HWIETheSecret

If it resonated with you,
it can probably help someone else.

Tag me in your posts on Twitter and Instagram.

Let's connect!

@ianthasinsight

Undecided

You know when you know what you know.

I'll never forget that Tuesday afternoon when one of my coworkers visited my classroom as I was preparing to leave for the day. She was always upbeat and positive, but that day, she had a different kind of pep in her step. When she entered the room, I had my head down at my desk, grading the last of a couple of stacks of papers. Her voice jolted me when she said, "Heeeeey, Ms. Ussin!"

I looked up from the papers, and as I always did with her, said, "Come on in. What's up?"

Hardly able to contain herself, she said, "There's someone I think you should meet."

Her smile was from ear to ear, and it was so contagious that I couldn't help but smile with her. She continued.

"He's a young man from New Orleans who wants to come and help out at the school with tutoring from time to time. He's a sharp brother! As soon as he said he was from New Orleans, I knew I had to introduce you two. Maybe you know some of the same people."

She shared a few more things that she'd learned about him. With a satisfied grin that confused me a bit at first, she told me she'd bring him by to meet me that Friday because he was scheduled to be back at the school. It wasn't until the very end of her jovial rant that I realized she was as excited as she was because she was hoping for a love connection. I don't know if it was because it was the end of the day and my brain was what we call "middle school fried" or because I'd been content and at peace with the Lord for years since *The Secret*, but I wasn't the least bit concerned about "love connecting" with anyone. Whatever the case, I hadn't linked her extra dose of energy to her intentions. I'd missed it completely. Once I connected the dots, we laughed it off together, and our conversation ended with her saying, "You never know what can happen."

She exited my classroom and threw me a wave.

That Friday, just as she said she would, my coworker escorted *Undecided* to my classroom and introduced us. We all made small talk for a few minutes, and then my coworker conveniently dismissed herself so *Undecided* and I could "get more acquainted". She giggled her way out of my room the same way she had a few days prior, letting her words trail off as she rounded the corner right outside my classroom door.

Undecided and I continued in conversation. We talked college talk—where we had completed our undergraduate studies, why he decided not to pledge into a fraternity and why I decided to pledge into a sorority, why he went on to graduate school to earn a master's degree right after undergrad and why I waited until after starting my career to work on my master's. We talked about where, exactly, in New Orleans we were from and learned that we attended rival high schools. That made for interesting banter because the rivalry was a longstanding one. We exchanged quite a few laughs reminiscing on things that only people who attended those schools would know. We talked about how our lives had led us to the Augusta area and what we enjoyed about the city. *Undecided* told me he hadn't been in Augusta a full year at that point, so he was still learning the place and looking forward to seeing what else it had to offer.

We covered a lot in that short talk. There was no "here's what you talk about when you first meet someone" stone unturned. You know how you just know good people when you meet them? You know how a conversation just has "I can talk to you about anything" chemistry? That's what we had, without a doubt. I felt like I was talking to someone I'd grown up with as we talked big-city talk about big-city things that Augustans wouldn't understand. Just that quickly, we'd already gained something that would be just ours. We'd scratched each other's homesick itch, and that's what helped us form an immediate connection. He reminded me of my high school guy classmates, the ones I deemed my brothers, who I joked with and talked to about other guys. The last thing on my mind was "becoming more acquainted" with *Undecided* like my coworker had hoped.

By the end of the conversation we'd exchanged phone numbers. The qualms I normally had with giving my number to someone I'd just met were nonexistent with him. I told him it was nice to have met him and to text if he needed anything. I meant, with every ounce of Southern belle in me, that he could text me if there was a need, even though I was sure he was self-sufficient and well able to care for himself. I didn't even expect to hear from him after that.

Nothing Serious

A couple of weeks later, I was at home, deep into my regular Friday night relaxation routine. I was sprawled out on my couch enjoying some mindless TV when my phone rang. It was *Undecided*. I answered in my humdrum, tired teacher tone, but his tone was the complete opposite. He had barely said ten words, and I was already exhausted from just listening to his chipper chatter. After a few exchanges of pleasantries to catch up from the only time we'd ever talked that day in my classroom, he jumped right in and asked if I'd accompany him to a semi-formal event *that* night. He said he'd considered not going but thought he shouldn't let the two tickets go to waste. I thought to myself, *Poor thing. He really doesn't know me. Everyone in my life knows what Friday night is for me; they know they have to catch me on Saturday if they expect me to be lively and have a good time.*

I didn't even have to think about my response to his invite. I said, "Don't you know it's Friday? I'm tired. I'm on my couch. I ain't goin' *nowhere* tonight."

He said, like only a New Orleans brother could, "Girl, get off that couch. You ain't *that* tired. C'mon now."

"And I have to wash my hair. My hair is dirty. I'm not prepared to be in semi-formal attire with my hair looking like this."

I had already pulled my hair out of the ponytail it had been in all week. It was tossed all about because, again, I had no plans to go anywhere.

"Girl, you know you know how to whip your hair up right quick. C'mon. Let's go. Pleeeease?"

"And who has a semi-formal dress, ready and waiting to be pulled out of the closet on a whim?"

"You know you do. You know y'all AKAs be ready. I know you got a dress you can put on. C'mon, now. Let's go. Pleeeease? I know you not gon' make me go by myself."

"Dude, I am not semi-formal event ready. I'm not leaving my house."

"Iantha. Girl. Get up and get ready so we can go. You know you wanna go. Go and get one of them AKA dresses and whip your hair up so we can go."

He did so much pleading and please-ing that I eventually just said okay.

After prying myself from the couch and settling in my mind that I was actually about to leave the comfort of my home to go to some hoity-toity event, I willed myself to find a dress, which, as *Undecided* had said, really wasn't too hard for me. Once I decided on the dress, I knew I could pull my hair up from my shoulders and back from my face into a style that would mask its need to be washed. I said a little prayer and asked the Lord for the energy to make it through the night. Then, I texted *Undecided* my address and prepared myself for a Friday evening away from the much-desired comfort of my home.

It turned out to be a pretty fun night because I was hanging out with a homeboy. We laughed a lot that night about everything and nothing. I spent the first maybe half hour of the night with *Undecided*, but it wasn't long before I was all over the room

192

catching up with fellow educators and other people I knew from around town. I checked in with *Undecided* periodically throughout the evening to make sure he was having as good a time as I was. He assured me he was. There were some heavy hors d'oeuvres and a little dancing, and after we'd had our fill of it all, we decided to call it a night. After the event, *Undecided* drove me home. We sat in his truck for a bit and rehashed the night before he walked me up to my apartment. He saw me in and headed home.

Undecided, an absolute Southern gentleman, was clean cut, boyishly good-looking, and always dressed for success. Even if he wore jeans, he was sure to have on a button-up, collared shirt that allowed him to at least throw on a bow tie and make the ensemble look like he cared about his appearance. And he *did* care. He was one of the few guys I knew who was unshakably intent on finding the right colored clothing to complement his milk chocolate complexion. I can't remember a time that he didn't look like he was ready to conduct business on the spot, with his astute-looking, thin-rimmed glasses and firm handshake to seal the deal. He was fresh out of grad school and brand spanking new on his first job in the technology field. The brother was ridiculously smart and accomplished, but being four years my junior, he was wet behind the ears in more ways than one. He felt more like a younger brother than anything. His biggest concern at that point in his life, and rightfully so, was figuring out if the Augusta area was where he wanted to settle. He was trying to determine if he wanted to work indefinitely in the particular line of technology where he was starting his career or if he wanted to broaden his scope. Then, there was the question of going back to school to pursue his doctorate. He didn't know if he wanted to do that right away or work a few years before diving back into student life. He was even questioning if he was ready to fully commit to adulthood, which was more evident in his actions than with his words.

Undecided was doing all the right things, giving attention to everything that any determined young professional would. Those life decisions were what mattered most to him in that season. A relationship was the least of his concerns, and I knew that. Yet, foolishly, I still allowed myself to get unnecessarily entangled in him.

After our night out at the semi-formal event, we texted daily and talked on the phone some too. We were definitely communicating more than I would have with any of my homeboys. *Undecided* was making check-in calls, letting me know all of his whereabouts, and that was strange to me. I certainly wasn't making check-in calls. In fact, some days, I was hoping he wouldn't call. He had more time on his hands than I did, and feeling like I needed to answer every time he called started to weigh on me a bit. I was a full-time teacher and student, working diligently on completing my master's degree requirements. I had obligations as the director of Praise Movement School of Dance and church responsibilities too, so I was a strict manager of my time. I didn't like spending it on anything that wasn't getting me closer to completing a necessary task or meeting a goal. But I surmised that maybe *Undecided* was calling so much because he didn't have an organic connection with anyone in the area like he did with me. So, I humored him.

We definitely had an easy connection. We learned we were strikingly similar in almost every way, but even with that, I just wasn't romantically attracted to him. It wasn't long before I began to feel like our conversations were going in circles. The small talk was draining, and it was eating up time that I could have been spending checking things off of my never ending "To Do" List. We were laughing at the same things and reflecting on the same moments we'd had in the little time we'd known each other. I kept waiting for more—for him to dig deeper to learn about who I was beyond all the surface stuff we'd already covered. And at that point, I was looking to learn the same of him because his behavior was raising questions. I kept saying to myself, *Hold on. This dude sure is calling and texting and wanting to hang around a lot. If he's gon' be in my space like this, I need to know his intentions. Is he trying to be more than just my brother-friend?*

As I mentioned before, because we connected like family, I'd instantly written him off as a potential love interest; I just couldn't see us being together in that way. Family-friendly was the nature of our relationship. Until things got confusing…

The Tables Turn

One Friday night, I remember feeling like the weight of the world had been lifted from my shoulders because I'd submitted my last major assignment of the semester. *Undecided* called, as he always did, and we talked our regular small talk. Surprisingly, though, about 15 minutes into the conversation, things took a turn. He started asking about my interests and was all of a sudden concerned about what I liked and didn't like. That led to us talking about music, and that opened up a whole new area of natural connection. We loved, literally, all the same music, and we loved it deeply. It was impossible to talk about our deep-rooted connections to specific songs and the memories attached to those songs without our conversation traveling back to New Orleans. Before I knew it, our music memories had us talking about our upbringings and our families and our friends and our schools and past relationships and a heap of other things until almost 5 AM. And even though we didn't say it, just like that, the tables had turned. An imaginary line had been drawn in the sand, and we crossed it and entered into a new space of being. Together. It was clear that things between us, from that point on, would never be the same.

A couple of months passed and the holiday season was upon us. It was Thanksgiving break for me, which meant a whole week off from school that I would be spending in New Orleans with my family. Thanksgiving happened to be *Undecided's* favorite holiday, so he took vacation time to be home in New Orleans too. Plus, he was terribly homesick. I didn't think we'd see each other while in our home city. I didn't imagine it was even a thought of his, but while there, he called and asked to take me out to a movie. I accepted the invite and told him he could pick me up from my parents' house.

Of course, the Southern gentleman was sure to arrive at my parents' house early enough to have a proper first meeting with them and still get us to our destination on time. My parents welcomed him in, and we all stood in the kitchen and talked. My mom had only a few things to say as she always did when first meeting the guys I brought home, but my dad was much different. He took over the conversation and engaged *Undecided* in man-to-man talk. My mom eventually disappeared, seemingly into thin air. I stepped away into the adjoining dining room when I noticed her absence. From afar, I listened as my dad asked probing questions to learn a little about *Undecided*, and I watched as he looked him over to detect his sincerity or lack thereof. Then, he made sure to ask what theater we were going to because even though I was grown and not even living under his roof anymore, he was still my dad and relentless protector.

Although I was only letting my parents *see* who *Undecided* was for their peace of mind because he was picking me up from their home, he'd done more than just be seen by them. He *met* them, which meant he had experienced a part of me that I didn't plan for and that linked us in a way I wasn't anticipating. Even if I didn't intend for it to forge something between us, it was inevitable, the very small something that it was. How could it not? He knew, just as much as I did, that his having met my family created "a knowing" that couldn't be erased. That, coupled with my not even thinking about kicking it with him while I was at home with my family, got my wheels turning. I wondered, *Why did he make it a point to take me out in New Orleans? How official is this date?*

I vividly recall, after returning home from the movies, going to my room and replaying every detail of our date in my mind. The first thing that grabbed my attention that night was that there had been some rain earlier in the day, so before we even got out of his truck, he said, "Let me make sure I get the umbrella just in case it's raining after the movie. I can't have you gettin' wet out here."

He reached behind my seat and grabbed his extra-large New Orleans Saints umbrella. Then, he got out and walked around to the passenger side to open my door. He took great care to ensure my step down from his high-off-the-ground Chevy Sierra was a careful one, chivalrously reaching out his hand to grab hold of mine. There were little puddles in the parking lot, so he led me as we walked, pointing out every puddle with his umbrella to make sure my feet missed every one. After purchasing our tickets, if there was a door to be opened, he opened every one for me, even if it meant he had to scurry past others to do it. Even the way he guided me to our seats had "this is my girl" written all over it. He was a step behind me, far enough to use his guard dog eyes to see what was in front of me and surrounding us, yet close enough to be able to swoop in at the slightest sign of danger. And then there was our pre-show talk. It was still amiable and fun loving, but there was a new tenderness to it. A "you are my only focus in this moment" tenderness. It all made me look forward to hanging out a little more when we got back to Georgia. I was anxious to see if the New Orleans *Undecided* would be present in Augusta.

In the months after that Thanksgiving break, if we weren't working—or I, fulfilling church or Praise Movement obligations—we were hanging out at my place or his. We prided ourselves in being wordsmiths, so we became instant word game buddies. We played Scrabble and Scattegories religiously, even scheduling our days around the games to see who would level up in our longstanding tournaments. We went out to see movies, and we stayed in to watch movies. I would cook and invite him over, and he would cook and invite me over. *Undecided* was a diehard Saints fan, like nothing I'd ever seen, so we watched every televised Saints game together that season. We just had good ol' fun!

I was comfortable with *Undecided*. I wasn't ready to share my deepest, darkest secrets with him or reveal all my hopes and dreams, but I trusted him on a level that was appropriate for the time I'd known him. He always kept his word. If he said he was going to swing by my place to hang out or just say hello, he did. If he said he was going to call, he called. If he said we were going somewhere, we went. And he was thoughtful. There were countless times when he would be out and about and see something he thought I'd want. He would call or text and ask if I'd like him to get it for me, especially if it was food or dessert.

Undecided wanted the best for me. Whenever we talked about my master's degree program and the stressors that came with going to school and working full time, he offered whatever help he could. Many times he graded my students' papers for me while I worked on grad school assignments. If there was ever a way he could lighten my load, he jumped in and did it. I never once felt like he had any ill will toward me. He was too gentle a soul for that. He wasn't doing things just to get in my good graces, and he wasn't making power moves to earn his way into my heart. I almost wished he had been, though, because at least that would have been less perplexing.

So, What *Is* This?

Undecided was comfortable with me too. Almost too comfortable. The kind of comfortable that's normally nonexistent in the suitor who's attempting to win a heart for potential companionship. I remember a couple times when he visited me at my place, very early into our getting to know each other. After having been in my home for only a few minutes, he'd taken off his shoes and propped his feet (one time bare) up on my couch. There were a couple of times, too, when we were in my kitchen talking and he opened my refrigerator and peered in to see if there was anything he could grab for a snack. When we would play board games, he would be ridiculously competitive, and no matter how much charm I threw out, he would not take it easy on me. Everything that screamed homeboy, I was getting it from him. He was doing things that my guy friends would've done, and things that my guy friends assured me they would never have done with someone they were trying to date. Not that soon anyway, no matter the chemistry.

Even though I was getting the friendship vibe from him, I just couldn't seem to separate that vibe from the "I want to be around you all of the time" energy he was emanating. I often thought, *What guy wants to be in his friend's space as much as he wants to be in mine?* My guy friends certainly didn't desire to be around me that much, and as I said, I have some that I consider to be brothers. We're close, but never did we go out on dates. We didn't hang out and talk over hours of Scrabble. We were certainly there for one another in times of need, but for the most part, we didn't rearrange our schedules for each other just to hang out simply because the other person wanted to. Nope. That wasn't how our friendships worked. But it was the norm with *Undecided*. So, yeah. There was the confusion. What the heck did he want from me? Why was he opening doors for me wherever we were whenever we were together? Why was he pulling out my seat or seeing me to my seat whenever we dined together? And why was his protective nature ten times that of the big sister protective mode I displayed when I first met him? Why was he calling to make sure I was home safely or talking to me my entire ride home from his apartment to ensure my well-being? Why was he volunteering to wash my car, something that outside of my dad and *The One,* no one—not even the guys I paid to wash it—had ever taken such pride in doing for me? Why was he offering to be my driver sometimes when I needed to handle business around town?

Mixed signals. Without a doubt.

My birthday rolled around, and if there was never anything confusing before, there was certainly some confusion then. For at least a week leading up to my birthday, *Undecided* kept asking what I was planning to do to celebrate. He told me on the Sunday afternoon before my Monday birthday that he was going to meet me at my apartment when I got off from work so he could take me to dinner. He asked that I let him know when I was headed home. I honored his request. After I was home for maybe 15 minutes, he knocked on my door. I was soon greeted with balloons, a small, personal chocolate cake, and a card. There may have been something else, now that I think of it, but those three things I vividly recall. The balloons, because they seemed to have lasted a lifetime, floating around my apartment. The card, because I love words and anytime someone takes the time to pick a card that speaks their thoughts toward me, I cherish them. The cake, because he knew I liked chocolate candy. He figured I must like chocolate cake too, which I don't care for as much, but the thought he put into choosing the cake was noteworthy. After I read the card that he requested be read in his presence, he insisted that we put candles in the cake so he could sing "Happy Birthday" to me. It was more for his amusement than for celebration because he'd bought trick candles. He took pictures of me reading the card and blowing out the candles and made sure I posed with the cake too because "you have to capture birthday memories," he said. I sincerely thanked him for his thoughtfulness and kindness, and we headed out to one of the new restaurants in town to enjoy dinner. There was no way I was going to let him tell me he didn't want more than friendship from me after that night.

I took some time to process my birthday deluge and refused to go any further without addressing my supposition. I needed to know *Undecided's* aim. I had to know, clearly, what he wanted from me, so one night I initiated the conversation. This was when I learned that any conversation requiring him to talk about the "us" that seemed to be forming would make him visibly uncomfortable. Every time. He pretty much always tried to conjure a way to steer the conversation in another direction. If ever he couldn't find a way, he'd get squirmy and spring up from wherever he was seated. Then he'd pace the floor. That night, he even clasped his hands together, forming an open circle into which he blew as if he were trying to warm them on a cold winter day. He just stood there and blew and searched for words to whatever question had been presented in our conversation. He couldn't answer. There appeared to be too much for him to unscramble in his brain. It was probably even more uncomfortable for him that night because I let him know in advance that we needed to talk; it didn't just happen naturally in conversation like other times. I didn't want to beat around the bush, so I straight up asked *Undecided*, "What are we doing? What, exactly, is going on with us?" And then came the antics.

He hopped up from the couch where we were sitting and walked to the opposite side of the room. He stood in one spot, and then the hand blowing began. His head dropped and his chin met his chest. For a minute, I said nothing. I didn't probe. I let him have his moment. When he came to, he walked back toward me and sat back down, defeat on his face. He knew there was no escaping the talk, so he gave himself over to it, hesitantly.

He let me talk, and I treaded lightly. I didn't ask any more questions because the first one had elicited all the theatrics. I did, however, take a few minutes to explain how his actions came across to me. I wanted him to understand that our "friendship" wasn't exactly what I considered to be friendship. I wanted him to understand that it was necessary for us to define our relationship. After I said all I needed to say, there was silence. He looked at me and then down at his hands. Then he looked at me again, and then back down at his hands. I could see he wasn't ready to be anything more than a friend even if he sometimes acted like he wanted more. He wasn't even able to articulate that, but his not being able to say it spoke loud and clear. His silence was my answer. He wanted to be known as my friend, but he wanted to be able to date me too. That wasn't what I wanted, though. I hadn't signed up for that. As far as I was concerned, if he was going to be my friend, he was going to be *just* my friend. Our time together and our interaction would have to have a whole new flow if he was to be *just* my friend. If he wanted to date me, then he was going to have to say that's what he wanted. The lines needed to be clear.

I thought *Undecided* would respond to what I'd said, or answer the question I asked at the top of the conversation, but that didn't happen. Instead, he slowly stood up and walked to the bathroom to have a moment to himself. I heard him run the water. I heard him taking deep breaths and pushing the air out with what sounded like frustrated sighs. It was really something. I just thought, *Wow. This really is hard for him.* But I didn't care. In the same wave of thought, I heard myself say, *Figure it out, bruh. We can't keep playin' around with this 'thang.*

When *Undecided* walked out of the bathroom, to my welcomed surprise, he actually spoke up, and that was all I'd ever wanted from him. I just wanted him to say what he was really thinking and feeling. He said, "I like us like we are. Slow and steady wins the race. We're building a good friendship. Let's just build our friendship first."

I responded in agreement. I told him we were definitely building a good friendship and that we should continue to build, but I told him we needed to back off and do it. I told him I liked hanging out with him but that I didn't do that much hanging out with friends. He was in too much of my space and taking up too much of my time, and if he wasn't going to be my man, I couldn't keep giving him that much of my attention. I didn't need to accept his date offers if we were just friends. I didn't need to spend hours on the phone with him. I didn't need to rearrange my schedule to just hang out with him because he wanted to spend time with me. I didn't need to encourage him along. I had a responsibility in what was going on with us too. If I knew he wanted to be just friends, I shouldn't have allowed him to try to make it more. We both had to make sure we were who we said we were in every way.

After our talk, or the strange semblance of such, *Undecided* reminded me that he was scheduled to head to Detroit that weekend with some friends and would be leaving in a couple of days. I told him to just enjoy his trip and not worry about calling or texting me. I told him he really didn't have to check in with me every time he went somewhere or even tell me he was going. My saying that seemed to stress him a little and make him feel like I was saying we couldn't ever talk again. It all seemed so final to him because of the conversation we'd just had. I had to ease him and tell him we could talk when he got back. I had to assure him it was okay and teach him at that moment, in brief, what friendship was supposed to look like. I really wanted him to see how he'd attached himself to the hip of our relationship.

He didn't call all weekend, and he didn't text, and because I knew how much we'd always talked and how much he always *wanted* to talk, I was sure it was tough for him. My notions were confirmed when he arrived late that Sunday evening in Augusta because the moment he landed, he called. I knew, then, that the poor guy was having his own struggle, and the Holy Spirit helped me to see it clearly. *Undecided* knew he wanted companionship, but he didn't want it in its fullness at that point in his life. He wanted to have relationship moments without the relationship commitment. He wanted to be with someone without *being* with them. And I knew it full well. He definitely cared for me. There was no doubt about that. Conversations we'd had let me know he wanted someone like me for a wife one day; he just didn't have an idea of when "one day" would be in his life. It was terribly difficult to watch every time he tried to communicate it. The confusion was apparent. As far as he was concerned, we could've hung out forever; he wouldn't have changed a thing. It was just too bad that I wasn't the "hang out" kinda girl. So, I pumped the brakes on how much time *Undecided* and I were spending together. We still hung out, and we still talked and texted, but not nearly as much as we had before. And I was cool with that.

Maybe a week or two after *Undecided's* Detroit trip, I was in prayer, and the Lord told me, clearly, that I was just gonna be "something *Undecided* did while he was in Augusta." I was a pastime that just happened to walk in on a chapter in his life that he needed help getting through. He didn't have any plans to stay in Augusta. In fact, over time, he began to loathe the place. If he wasn't required to complete so much time on his job before he could uproot, he wouldn't have stayed as long as he had. I, on the other hand, knew the Lord had called me to Augusta, and I loved my set place. I wasn't going anywhere. God showed me there was no way *Undecided* would be able to commit himself to a relationship without knowing what he wanted for "us". He wasn't going to be able to do anything for "us" because he didn't yet know what he wanted for himself. God told me I didn't need to desire anything more than friendship with *Undecided*. He told me to detach my emotional involvement so I could protect my heart. That should have been easy to do since He'd given me direct insight to let me know there was nothing there, but I didn't detach. At least not as much as I should have.

Iantha Ussin

The Writing on the Wall

I'm sure you're wondering, "Iantha, how can you see in *Undecided's* actions that he just wanted to be friends, hear it from his mouth, *and* hear it directly from God and *still* hang around?" I get it. I asked myself too. That should have been the time I put up boundaries to show *Undecided* what our relationship would be from that point on. I could've declined date invites. I could've easily ignored phone calls and text messages. I knew how not to answer. But why was I *still* trying to figure out if he wanted more when I knew he couldn't handle more? And not only that, I knew there were things about him that didn't even agree with my lifestyle, like his drinking. Why was I trying to look past that with him when I knew I would never date anyone who drank, and especially not anyone who drank to drunkenness? There I was, though, knowing that *Undecided* was drinking often enough for the Lord to confront me about it, and I still stood around and watched.

I kept telling myself, as *Undecided* was undoubtedly telling himself, that he knew when to turn his drinking off. He was a working professional who knew he couldn't drink heavily during the week, and he didn't drink every weekend, so he was good, right? And he'd only had drinks a few times in my presence, so he respected me, right? Yeah, sure. But I knew of multiple instances when he had been drinking outside of our time together and made poor, almost life-altering decisions. I knew if he'd made poor decisions as a result of his drinking when he *wasn't* with me, it would only be a matter of time before he would when he *was* with me. Still, though, I looked past what was right before me. Maybe I chose "not to see" because we'd built such a good friendship before I knew he was a drinker. Maybe I was trying not to judge and focused my attention on leading by example with my drink-free life. Whatever the case and whatever my reason, I was unnecessarily entangled, and God used an actual spider to show me the web I was in.

One Saturday, when *Undecided* left my apartment after one of our Scrabble tournaments, I was sitting on my couch preparing my mind to begin a homework assignment. I was about to reach down and grab my laptop from the floor, but before I could, my eyes caught a black spider sitting right in the middle of my chest, a stark contrast to the plain white blouse I was wearing. There was no way I could miss it. I screamed and jumped up from the couch and flicked the spider off of me all in one whip. My tan carpet helped me see where the spider landed, and in a nervous, but determined frenzy, I took a step and smashed it. Where in the world had it even come from? I had never seen a spider in my apartment and I had been living there for years.

I sat back down, heart beating like a snare, and the Holy Spirit spoke. He told me I was tightly wound in a spider's web and I didn't even have to be; I *wanted* to be there. He spoke just as distinctly as He had when He told me I was simply going to be something *Undecided* did while he was in Augusta. He told me I had woven a web and laid myself right in it. It would have been too easy, especially for someone like me, to cut "relationship ties" with *Undecided* as I had done so easily with the guys who aren't featured in this book. Those guys never even made it past "hello". I read them at first sight and never even allowed things to progress. I knew they would be a waste of my time, so I didn't even allow them to enter into my space. Oooh, but *Undecided*...

The whole ordeal was a mess. It was downright stupid for me to hang around like I did, and I still don't even understand *why* I did. Every time I thought on it in years past, all I came up with was that I must've enjoyed having someone around just as much as he did. Maybe he was filling an empty space for me as I was for him. There's no other explanation because I wasn't impressed with anything *Undecided* could offer me. I didn't care that he was making crazy money in the technology field. I didn't care that he had degrees. I didn't care about any of his accolades. I genuinely enjoyed *him*. We had fun together, and we had so much in common. I really think I let little things like that cloud my judgement. I would still take every one of his actions and analyze them like we women do. I would think he was making moves, but, of course, as I've already established pretty clearly, he wasn't.

If I haven't learned anything else, I've learned that a year goes by really quickly in situationships. When I went back to my journals to look at dates and timelines for this book, I couldn't believe I'd spent an entire year going back and forth within myself about *Undecided* before I resolved to finally take things at face value. I realized that we can be unknowingly overly engrossed in the unique mix of actually enjoying the newness of the situationship that we don't yet know is a situationship, and trying to figure out if the situationship, that we don't know is a situationship, is developing into a relationship. When we look up one day, realizing we've been in that mix for six months, it dawns on us that we are, in fact, in a situationship. Then, when we decide to have "the conversation" and try to allow it more time to see if things will turn around, we discover that another four or five months have passed. Then we know it's time to revisit that conversation again because either things have changed and it's time to go to the next level, or things haven't changed much at all and it's time to call it quits.

That was certainly my story. I looked back and realized I'd lived it with *Rebound* and *The Secret*, and it was happening again with *Undecided*. Throughout the months after *Undecided's* Detroit trip, I had a few more revelations outside of all that God was showing me in plain sight, but the next Thanksgiving was it for me. I'd stayed too long, and I knew it. I'd put myself in my sorry predicament, and I knew it. I'd been confused because of my own doing. It was just time to let it all go.

Just as we'd done a year prior, both *Undecided* and I traveled separately to New Orleans to be with our families for

Thanksgiving. Naturally, because we'd grown so much in our situationship, and because we were together all the time, I thought surely we would hang out again in New Orleans, but we didn't. I thought surely I'd meet his family, but that didn't happen either, which made me feel cheated in a sense because he'd met my family.

The day after Thanksgiving, my sister-in-law, niece, and I attended the infamous Bayou Classic Battle of the Bands between Grambling State University and Southern University. It had been years since any of us had gone, so I was really looking forward to it. I had told *Undecided* earlier in the week that we'd be going, and he said he and his cousins would be going too. With an event as huge as the Battle of the Bands, in the mega New Orleans Superdome, there was no way I ever thought I would see him, but when we got to our seats, *Undecided* texted me and told me to look up. He and his cousins were five rows above us. We both laughed at how strangely coincidental that was. We texted some throughout the event, and at some point I expected that he would ask me to hang back a few minutes at the end of the show so we could say hello, like we actually knew each other on as deep a level as we did and because we hadn't seen each other at all that week. I thought maybe I'd meet his cousins, and he my niece and sister-in-law, but he never asked me to stay back. At that point, with my trying to accept him just wanting to be friends while still deciphering the mixed signals that "said" otherwise, I most certainly wasn't about to make the move and add to the confusion. When my sister-in-law, niece, and I were leaving, I distinctly remember wondering if *Undecided* and I were in a situation similar to the one I'd been in with *The Secret*. I started to question if my introducing him to my niece and sister-in-law would've made him feel uncomfortable. I wondered if it was something that I even needed to concern myself with. It was that thinking that made me stop and say, *Uhn uhn, Iantha. We've been here. If we have to wonder if it's "okay" to introduce him to family, or if we have to hint at meeting family, this ain't it.*

I was fine when we left the Battle of the Bands, but by the time we made it home, I was in a funk. I separated myself from my family for a bit so I could think. I had to process what had been happening in that year's time. I had to process how different that Thanksgiving was from the one before it. I had to rifle through my deep-rooted, true feelings about it all, and I had to literally take a look in the mirror and ask myself why I was doing what I was doing to myself. Why had I allowed myself to get so ensnared? Why was I hanging on so tightly to *nothing*? How had I let myself end up in that place? Again! Aargh! I had been deceived. And not so much by *Undecided* as by my own thoughts and feelings and what ifs and maybes. Sure, he said one thing and showed something different in many respects and on many occasions, but I *knew* what **GOD** was showing me, and that should've been the final say.

I was so angry with myself for letting it happen. I was hurt and frustrated and embarrassed. I hated that I'd ignored all of God's warnings and instead trusted small glimmers of "deceptive" hope from *Undecided*. I ignored warnings from my best friend, my mom, and even my dreams, which I'll discuss further in *Understanding Undecided*. I felt like I'd hurt the heart of God, and like I'd let myself down. I'd become the dumb girl, and my pride wasn't too happy about having to walk in her shoes. I cried like a baby that night.

My brother and sister-in-law were leaving my parents' house to head home that next morning. I was sad they were leaving because we'd had such a good time and I always miss them terribly, but the feeling of having to see them go was coupled with the swarm of emotions that was already brewing inside of me. When it was time to say goodbye, I hugged my sister-in-law, collapsed in her arms, and burst into tears. I couldn't even tell her what was happening. I was too ashamed. Too hurt. Too outdone.

Decided

Not long after my family left, *Undecided* called. I hesitated answering but decided to pick up. After some small talk, I told him I was planning to head back to Georgia later that day, which surprised him because I wasn't due to leave until the following day. I needed the drive, though. I was the kind of frustrated that needed hours of inactivity and nothingness so I could clear my head and pray and cry again if necessary. I had to get out of the space that connected me to my recent discovery. The crushing epiphany was just too much. I knew I wouldn't forget, but I sure didn't want to swim in the newness of it.

He said, "Noooooo. Don't go. You don't have to go back to work yet. Why are you leaving so soon?"

That gave me permission to switch gears and take the conversation another way. He was completely unaware of the time I'd spent the night before in my own thoughts, sifting through my feelings, and he had no clue about my personal introspective discovery, but that didn't keep me from forging forward to dig into his psyche concerning what I'd just unveiled. He appeared to be very passionate about me staying one extra day, so I asked him why he wanted me to stay. I followed the question with a statement that rang in my mind for months thereafter. I said, "If you give me a reason to stay, I'll stay."

The saddest, yet most comforting thing was already knowing, before he even opened his mouth, that he didn't have an answer for me. If that man wanted to be with me, he would have compelled me to stay, and I knew it full well, but I knew he wouldn't be able to give me a reason to stay. I knew he *couldn't*. But I wanted him to squirm, and I wanted him to struggle to answer because it would make it that much easier for me when I'd need to point back to that conversation to dismiss him from my life.

I wish I could do a replay of how nervous he was when he spoke his next words. I wish I could make you hear the fight in his voice and the uncomfortable silences between his words. Oh, it was awful!

He said, "Well...don't you want to stay with your family? I mean...you know you don't get to see them often."

The first uncomfortable silence followed those words as he searched for more to say. And I let him labor. I held the phone to my ear and looked off into the distance.

"Don't you want to enjoy your mom's good cooking?"

He wanted a response to that question. He paused and waited for it. I held my peace, still staring off, hearing him, but not even considering answering.

He reached way down for his next words.

"It's technically still Thanksgiving as long as there are leftovers."

There was another silence. I finally decided to speak after that one. I told him I'd gotten my fill of my family and I was good. I told him I could cook my own food at home. I showed about as much enthusiasm as paint slowly drying on a wall, and he sensed it. He knew I was searching him.

"Is there any other reason I should stay?" I asked.

He clammed up like he was being asked to stand naked on stage before a sold-out crowd. The childlike fear in his tone and in those weird silent moments told me he didn't want to say the wrong thing, but that he was too afraid to say the right thing because either way, he would be in trouble. And it was noted. It was the final note for me too. I didn't need anything else.

I said my goodbyes to my family a few hours later, got in my car, and took the surprisingly peaceful 8½-hour ride back to Augusta. It was all I needed to reset. I didn't talk to *Undecided* anymore while he was in New Orleans. He called. I didn't answer. He texted. I didn't respond. I'd entered that Iantha numb stage, and I was planning our finale. I just needed him back in Georgia so I could deliver the last act.

I knew a talk was too much for him, and quite frankly, I didn't want to talk, so just as I had done with *The Secret* so I would know I was being heard, I wrote *Undecided* a letter and mailed it to him. Our "finale" was understood. I texted him a few days after I thought he should've gotten the letter just to ensure he'd received it, and he confirmed that he had. The letter asked him to respond if he felt he needed to, and a few days after receiving my text, he *did* respond. I didn't care though. When I sent the letter, it didn't matter to me if I heard back from him or not because I knew…

He wasn't it either.

Understanding *Undecided*

Just let it be what it is.
Don't try to make it what it's not.

There's more to be revealed about *Undecided*. Some things I chose to leave out of the situationship recap so I could talk about them more in depth here.

Understanding Undecided #1 – If he can't define the relationship, walk away.

I've said this already, but I can't say it enough. When a man knows what he wants, he **shows** it first, and then he backs it up by saying so. If he doesn't want something, the same is true. He'll show it first, and sometimes, he'll say it too. If he's not able to clearly say that he wants the relationship, he doesn't want it. Walk away. And just trust me on that.

Understanding Undecided #2 – Ask the uncomfortable, but very necessary questions up front.

Why are we afraid to do this? When things aren't looking right, ask questions. When things aren't feeling right, ask questions. Don't wait until you're wrapped up in the emotion of "being together" because it clouds your judgement and makes it harder to address important matters. Ask first, feel later. Use wisdom with your asking.

Understanding Undecided #3 – You have to care about him enough to let him go so he can grow.

Have you ever eaten a piece of fruit that wasn't ripe? How about a piece of meat that was undercooked? Ever dated a man who hadn't yet developed into all he desired or was created to be? All the same. Not an enjoyable experience and can surely make you sick.

God showed me *and* straight up told me that *Undecided* wasn't ready for anything more than friendship. Even though I was getting mixed signals from him, thinking that maybe things would come around because he was clearly into me, I knew the truth. I knew he was young and developing and needed time to grow. And guess what? You know too. We all know when a man isn't ready for a relationship. Unfortunately, though, more times than not, we try to make him ready, which does nothing but cause us headache and sometimes heartache in the end. So let me help you...

When you see a man isn't ready for a relationship (especially when he says it), don't try to make him ready. Let him go so he can ripen and develop in whatever area he feels he needs to develop. He needs time to figure himself out so he can feel like a man, because if he doesn't feel like a man, he won't present like one, he won't perform like one, and he won't produce like one. Give him to the Lord. Let God complete the work He started in that man.

I remember talking to *Undecided* one time about "us," and he said something like, "You know Augusta is where you want to be. You like it here and you're set in your career. I'm not. I don't wanna stay here, and I have other things I still want to do."

He was telling me, without telling me, that he didn't have what he felt he should have to bring to the table for an "us". He was telling me, without telling me, that he wasn't yet the man he thought I needed. He was telling me that he needed time to develop and grow and plan and build, and he knew he couldn't do a relationship *and* develop and grow and plan and build. The two couldn't coexist.

And, ladies, this is where we mess it up. We think it's so cute and "ride or die" to try to build with him, to help him out, and to be patient with him while he grows, when in most cases, he never even asks for that. In fact, most times, he expresses the exact opposite desire. He wants to develop alone so he can later present himself as ready to the woman he chooses. It all goes back to letting the man seek you out and tell you that he's ready for a relationship. When he's ready, he'll be clear. If he's not clear, he ain't ready, and you don't have to sit around and "eat unripe fruit". Don't make yourself sick. Let it go so it can grow.

Understanding Undecided #4 – Don't ignore the signs.

Let's talk the real. When you're getting to know a potential love interest and he invites you into his intimate spaces like his car or his home, you take extra special care not to get too comfortable at first. You're mindful of barriers because you have common courtesy and general human respect. Even when entering into a friendship and you're just hanging out and getting to know a person, you don't go into his/her living space and make yourself at home. We all know that when someone says "make yourself at home," it comes with an unspoken understanding that we're not going to pull back the covers on their bed and lie in it. We're not going to open their drawers and pull out undergarments and excuse ourselves to the bathroom to put them on. We don't get that loose with people upon first meeting them, and especially not with a potential love interest. In fact, truth is, we all fake it a little at first. We put our best foot forward. Even in our being true to who we are, there are still some curtains we keep drawn because there are things we're just not ready to reveal. And that's safe. It's cautionary.

There *is* a comfort that's easier to get to with friends, though, and that's the comfort that was obvious with *Undecided*. He was operating in "friend comfort" from the very beginning, and it was loud and clear, but I ignored the sign.

I've already shared how *Undecided* would take off his shoes and prop his bare feet up on my couch, and how he would walk right into my kitchen and open the refrigerator and look for food, but what I didn't reveal is how he would visit me sometimes for the sole purpose of using my computer because he didn't have one at the time.

Now, I don't know a lot of things, but there are some things, as my pastor says, that I just know in my knower. And one thing I know is there's a pride that comes in a man's DNA that says, *Even if I don't have it, it ain't her business to know I don't.* In a man's eyes, if it's revealed to a woman of interest that he doesn't have what he needs to take care of himself, it's like telling her that he can't take care of her. And if it's his plan to have her for himself, the last thing he wants her to see is that he can't meet his own basic physical, emotional, and professional/career needs.

Everything in me knew that my brother, or any one of my male cousins or friends, would never let a woman of interest know he didn't possess the basic tools he needed to perform his work— especially if he, like *Undecided*, was a professional, licensed technological engineer with many a professional accolade and technological engineering pay. And if he *did* reveal that he didn't have something as basic as a computer, which was a minimum essential for *Undecided's* line of work, he certainly wouldn't have been at a potential love interest's home using her computer to do his work. He would've used a friend's or even gone to the public library before he did that. Let her see that he had to use her things to take care of his business? Absolutely not! And especially not in the early stages of their time together.

This screamed so loudly at me, but I ignored it too. I definitely appreciated his honesty, but it was an honesty that a man who was after me wouldn't have given right up front.

Just like me, there are some things you just know in your knower. You know when he's constantly stepping away to make and take phone calls in another room, something's up. Don't ignore that sign. You know when you haven't met any of his friends or family after all the time you've been kickin' it, something's up. Don't ignore that sign. You know if he's skating around conversations and isn't forthright with basic information, something's up. Don't ignore that sign. If you are a woman of

God, you have an advantage. You have the Holy Spirit. He causes us to see what we wouldn't be able to without His help. Don't ignore Him. Learn from my failure and the consequences I suffered as a result. DO NOT ignore the signs.

Understanding Undecided #5 – Don't ignore the people who matter most in your life when they point out red flags. Most times they can see what you can't.

My Best Friend

Remember how my best friend visited me for a week when I was "with" *The Secret?* Years later, she visited me for a week when I was "with" *Undecided.* She had seen the foolishness that happened with *The Secret*, but she didn't have much to say about it. In fact, to this day, she says that whole time was a blur. She doesn't remember any particulars; she only remembers how it all felt. She remembers that time feeling vague and dark and heavy. She says it was cloudy. Things weren't as cloudy with *Undecided*, but there were definitely some semblances. When she looked me in my eye as I talked about *Undecided*, and she heard and felt some of the same things she'd heard and felt with *The Secret*, she couldn't keep her peace. She refused to be silent again.

I was embarrassed to have been with *The Secret*, so I didn't talk much about him. I hid most of him from her sight. *Undecided* was "my friend," though, so I talked openly about the fun he and I were having together. I talked about our night out in New Orleans and how my parents had met him. I talked about how we played games and watched movies all the time. I told her how he never made any sexual advances at me and how I felt like he was the perfect gentleman. I went on and on about how much we had in common too. I built a case, thinking she'd give her stamp of approval, but that wasn't (and isn't) how our accountability worked. We asked each other the hard questions. All of what I'd said was well and good, and I'd painted quite the picture, but my best friend wanted to know where *Undecided* stood in his walk with the Lord, *if* he had one. She wanted to know about his character. She wanted to know if he was the man of God who embodied the qualities that I'd always envisioned in my one-day husband. And she wanted to know these things only because she could see I was smitten and desiring a relationship even though I'd said we were just friends. She saw right past my cover-up talk. My best friend reminded me of my standard, the very standard God had set for me. If I was considering connecting with *Undecided* in exclusivity, there would have to be some non-negotiable common ground, and that common ground would have to be the firm foundation that is Jesus Christ. She kept that before me and let that frame our conversation. We could talk about fun and games after that.

When I didn't have a clear answer for her about where *Undecided* stood in his walk with Jesus, our conversation got awkward. I couldn't say anything about *Undecided's* relationship with the Lord because I didn't know if he had one. I knew he went to church sometimes, and that was about it. When I would ask him about church and what he was learning, the conversations were always choppy and quick. He'd hit on some high points from a sermon, and that would be it. If I asked him to expound, he couldn't. If I asked him to talk about how the sermon applied to his life, I wouldn't get much there either. His conversation nor his life reflected a fruitful, flourishing relationship with God.

After explaining that to my best friend, I could see she was really having a hard time understanding what was going on with me. In her eyes, it was like I was a different person. She'd seen me, multiple times, handle my business with cutting guys off—the guys who wanted my time but clearly weren't worth it—the guys who didn't want to live a life for Christ. In those instances, it was "hi" and "goodbye". I had earned a reputation for quickly seeing past foolishness, so it was a bit disconcerting for her to see me wrapped up in the foolishness I abhorred. It caught her (and me, honestly) completely off guard to see it not only once with *The Secret*, but twice with *Undecided*.

To squelch some of the awkwardness that hung in the air between us as we talked that day, my best friend asked to see pictures of *Undecided*. She said, "Is he on Facebook?" I told her he was, so we got up from my couch and walked over to the adjoining dining room to the computer. I was uncomfortable because I knew what was there, but with our commitment to accountability, I knew there could be no secrets. We were faithful to full disclosure, so onto his Facebook page we went.

There *Undecided* was, in a picture that someone had tagged him in, laid out on the floor in someone's apartment, face pressed into the carpet, drunk, as the caption had pointed out. And there he was again, in another picture that *he* posted, grinding on some girl at a party. And there were other pictures of him posed professionally and lovingly with coworkers and family, but, of course, what stood out were the first two pictures. They'd been taken a couple years prior but were nonetheless currently incriminating. I tried to explain the actions in the pictures away. I tried to explain that it wasn't the present him and only a small fraction of who he was, but there was no escaping the truth. I knew he could still get that drunk, so my defense was pointless and unconvincing because even *I* didn't believe it. And who knew what he did at parties and other outings when he wasn't with me? Grinding on girls could have been a normal thing. I didn't know.

I made talk of his pictures with coworkers and family, trying to convince my best friend, and myself, again, that there was something—anything—that made *Undecided* worthy of my time and attention, but it wasn't working. I was finally being faced with the truth of our situationship from someone on the outside who could look in and see what I'd chosen not to see, and I felt cornered. I wanted to be justified in my actions. I wanted it to be okay for me to want to be with him. I wanted there to be something, but I'd known all along that there wasn't, and that there never would be.

My best friend didn't challenge me right away, but written all over her face was *Iantha, really? Are you seriously trying to make this okay?* I later learned that she didn't even know what to say at first. She was engulfed in trying to determine what had come over me. She and I had always talked about (and still do) how too many godly women try to make relationships happen with "good men" who aren't godly men because they believe they can cause those men to change. Some women lay down their standards, get impatient, and settle because they just want someone around. She was afraid I was doing that, and she didn't know how to tell me that I was doing what we'd always prayed other women wouldn't. This was not who she knew me to be. I didn't play that "try to help him along" foolishness and that "sometimes they just need a godly example" mess. But that's exactly how it was playing out, and it was hard for her to watch. It was one of the roughest patches in our friendship. She knew she couldn't *make* me do anything, but she wasn't going to let me go on without warning.

Later, she challenged me. She called me out on the carpet like she's supposed to do and as she's done every time it was necessary throughout the course of our friendship. She didn't beat me down into condemnation, but she spoke the truth and called out the lies. She asked me what I, a spirit-filled believer, had in common with someone who obviously wasn't.[16] She pointed out how different our lives were and how two people can't walk together except they agree.[17] One thing she said that stuck with me in a way that I couldn't shake was, "Iantha, I can't even imagine being in relationship with someone who can't even cover me in prayer. He

---

[16] II Corinthians 6:14-15 & verse 17, *Holy Bible*

[17] Amos 3:3, *Holy Bible*

can't even take life's issues and concerns to the Lord and cover you. What kind of relationship would that be if he can't cover y'all?"

Oh, she definitely waved that red flag to caution me, and she left it up to me to decide while she took it all to the Lord in prayer. I played around a little while longer with *Undecided* after that week with my best friend, but you better believe her words and the look in her eyes never left me.

My Mom

My mom and I have a good relationship. I know I can talk to her about anything. Anything but relationships. You see, when I moved to Augusta at the tender age of 23, and in her mind, fresh out my relationship with *The One* (because to her, *Rebound* didn't count), she was asking all the time if I was dating and who I was dating, and if there was any other query that was along the lines of dating, she asked that too. I think she was even asking about marriage. It wasn't the only thing she asked about or that we talked about, but *every time* we talked, she asked, and it got to be too much. I had to lovingly and respectfully ask her to leave it alone. I had to ask her to let *me* be the one to let her know when I had someone in my life who I felt was worthy of her and my dad knowing about. I wasn't telling them about people who I couldn't see a future with. I didn't want them meeting just anyone. I wanted them to meet my husband. My request took her by surprise, but she obliged and never asked again.

My situationship with *Undecided* was a unique case because of him having picked me up from my parents' house, so my mom knew about him. Because of that, naturally, I expected that at some point she'd ask some follow-up questions about the time we were spending together in Georgia. I didn't mind the questions and conversation. I filled her in on what I thought was necessary, and from that, because my mom is my mom, and because she's been around the block a time or two, aaaaand because she knows her daughter, she was able to tell me when I was with her on an extended visit to New Orleans that something wasn't right.

I had been in New Orleans a few days by the time she and I fell into a conversation about *Undecided*. My mom noticed that I hadn't said anything about him, and she wondered why. She wondered if he was in New Orleans at that time and if I would be missing any time with our family to be with his family. When I told her I wasn't planning on seeing him because we just hadn't talked about it, the conversation took a turn.

"And you haven't met *anyone* in his family? *Nobody*?" she asked, stunned. She just *could not* believe it.

In the next breath, with every bit of her New Orleans vernacular, she broke it down to me. The words rushed from her as if they'd been held up for years, waiting to be released.

"I know you might not wanna hear this, but I'm ya mama, and I'm just gon' tell you how I see it. It don't look like he want nothin'. He just wanna hang out. If he wanted to be in a relationship, he woulda made some moves by now. He ain't serious. And you shouldn't want to be hangin' around with somebody who ain't serious about you. I think he's a nice lil' fella and all, and he got some things goin' for himself from what you tell me, but he don't' want nothing witchu. He just hangin' around. He want a friend."

And I knew she was right. At that point, God had already told me. *Undecided* had already told me. My best friend had pointed out how unequally yoked we were. I honestly didn't need anyone else to point it out.

We talked about a few more things concerning *Undecided*. My mom said, "And you mean to tell me he never tried to kiss you?"

She awaited my response, chin to her chest, eyes bucking at me over her glasses.

"I don't care how respectful a man is about boundaries, if he's interested in you and attracted to you, you would've gotten some kind of advance from him. Somethin' just ain't right. He don't want nothin' serious. He is wastin' your time, Iantha."

My mom *always* tells it like it is, and in her observations of all my relationships throughout my life, she has never been wrong. Never. Although there was a whole bunch of the motherly "I know you ain't draggin' my daughter along" going on, there was even more of "he's just not that into you" in there. And I knew she was right.

Undecided never did anything but hug me, and barely that. I was glad about it, for the most part, because it made any fight with temptation pretty much non-existent. There was no pull of physical attraction between us, and it wasn't because he wasn't good looking or didn't have a nice physique. All of that was there. The same was true for me. I knew I was an all-around catch, but because there was no desire on his part to be anything more than friends, he wasn't putting out any vibes for our physical attraction to ignite.

My mom waved the red flag and cautioned me because she was able to focus in on what my blurry vision was having a hard time seeing. I knew there was nothing there to hold on to, but I didn't listen and wasted more time just hangin' around.

Understanding Undecided #6 – Don't ignore the dreams the Lord sends you.

I've always been a dreamer, but it wasn't until I gave my life to the Lord that I understood God was speaking to me through my dreams. When I studied the life of Joseph in the Bible and saw similarities in not only the types of dreams we had, but in our ability to interpret them, I knew I needed to learn more and sit at the feet of others who were well versed in God's communication through dreams. The more I studied God's Word and other books written by giants in the faith, and the more I prayed, the more I dreamed and the clearer my dreams became. God showed me that dreams would be yet another way for Him to give me vision, revelation, and warning. And so He did.

You already know that while I was in the situationship with *Undecided*, God was speaking loud and clear in my prayer time. He was speaking through my best friend and my mom and even a couple other people who I'd talked to about us. I was hearing God's warnings through my pastor's sermons too, but I ignored it all. Before long, God began to bombard me with dreams, literally every night, because I wasn't listening any other time. He wanted my undivided attention, and He knew He could get it while I was asleep. Three of those dreams were so vivid, so telling, and so gripping that they never left me. At that point in my life, I was writing all of my dreams down. I could have very well not have written these three down and still remembered every detail.

Dream #1

Undecided and I were talking in my apartment. I was sitting on the couch, and he was kneeling on the floor, facing me. He had a cardboard box that sat in the palm of one of his hands. The other hand was pressed down on the top of the box, holding the lid closed. As he talked to me, smiling from ear to ear, he sat up on his knees and slowly moved the box from side to side and in a circle and from side to side again. He wanted me to think he was about to perform a magic trick, so he took on a magician's role with his antics. After about a minute of his grand display of abracadabra, he sat the box on the floor right in front of him. With one hand, he removed the lid and simultaneously reached down into the box with his other hand and grabbed hold of a black snake. I was horrified that he had a snake in his hand, but on his face was sheer delight. I scooted to the far end of the couch, as far away from him as I could. He had the snake by the tail, spinning it around and around above his head as if it were a lasso. He threw his head back and just laughed and laughed, and I, pressed into the arm of the couch, just watched.

Animals are symbolic in dreams. Snakes symbolize, as they do in the Bible, the enemy, evil, and anything contrary to godliness. The Lord showed me, immediately upon waking from that dream, that *Undecided* wasn't yet done with the thrill of living on the edge with reckless activity. He showed me, too, that if I continued to hang around with *Undecided*, it wouldn't be long before carnality would invade my life, because in the dream, *Undecided* had brought "the display" into my home (my personal space). The interpretation was clear as day, and the truth of it was evidenced in many ways.

I'll never forget waking up one Saturday morning to four missed calls from *Undecided*. The calls had been placed within minutes of each other, and they were all in the 4 AM hour. When I spoke with him later that day, I asked him if he'd meant to call me all those times at that hour. He confirmed he had. My next question, of course, was why. He said he'd been out with some friends and had lost the keys to his apartment. He was hoping he could find refuge on my couch.

I knew, without a doubt, again, that *Undecided* didn't see me as anything more than a friend. No man who is looking to have anything serious with a woman would reveal his lack of responsibility so freely. It was so matter of fact for him. No shame whatsoever. If a man was trying to secure a future with me, the last thing he would want me to see was that he had lost his keys and couldn't get into his own home. He was living like he was still in college. It was clear he didn't want to turn away from what he considered to be fun, but what I and anyone else with any adult sense saw as reckless. There was no doubt he'd been drinking that night and was probably so drunk he couldn't place his keys. I wouldn't be surprised, thinking on it now, if the keys had been right in his pocket.

God used the dream and its meaning to help me connect the dots in the spirit to what I was actually seeing and experiencing with *Undecided*. It was a dream of confirmation and warning.

Dream #2

Over the years, one thing I've learned through prayer and study is that when God sends a dream, the emotions we feel in the dream are real. He uses the emotions to capture our attention so we can key in on that particular part of the dream for the message. The emotions in this dream were unbelievably apparent.

I never met *Undecided's* mother, but I'm pretty sure he once showed me a picture of her. Even though I'd seen the picture, I didn't lock her face into my memory. I couldn't confidently say I knew what she looked like, but in this dream, I saw her clearly, and the face in the dream, be it hers or not, I'll never forget.

Undecided had invited me to his family's home with him. We were very much together and I was looking forward to getting to know him through his family. We arrived at his parents' house in a taxi, and when we got out, my excitement instantly turned to dread. I could literally feel my shock and disbelief in the dream because I knew before we even walked up the long sidewalk that led to his parents' front door that his mom knew nothing about me. The weirdest thing was that I didn't sense any of it in the taxi just minutes prior. There had been a knowing within me that *Undecided* and I had already talked about being at his family's house. There had been a knowing within me that his family was aware of my coming, but when I was walking up to that house, I was flooded with the contrary. His mom didn't have a clue I was accompanying her only son whom she loved so much. I knew my presence would not be received well.

When we walked into the house, it was quiet. No one was downstairs. His mom had heard the door open and close, so she started down the stairs and stopped about halfway when she saw us. *Undecided* and I were standing at the door, and his mom stood on the stairs with one arm down by her side and the other resting on the banister. She glared at me like, *Who are you?* She said nothing to me, and *Undecided* said nothing at all, to her or to me. He didn't even greet his mom. There was no "Hey, Mom" or a rush to the stairs to give her a hug. He just walked off to the left toward what appeared to be the kitchen and left me standing there, looking at his mom while she stood on the staircase looking at me. His walking away was understood as, *Well, alright. You go ahead and deal with whatever she's about to tell you. You're on your own.*

As she made her way toward me, I looked at her with hopes of softening her countenance with my charm and win-over personality, but she walked right past me, rolled her eyes as she passed, and went toward the kitchen where her beloved son was.

Later in the dream, more of his family had come over to the house. Everyone was having a good time. I'd actually made some "love connections" with other members of the family. I felt welcomed by them. As the day progressed, I had conversations with everyone in the house except his mom. There were conversations happening where every person in the room contributed, and she would talk to everyone at some point, but she intentionally never said anything to me. We played a game where literally everyone in the house was involved. I remember it being her turn to pass an object to someone so the game could move along, and the object had to be passed across the room. It made sense for her to pass it to me because I was closest to the person it was going to, but she refused to hand it to me. She passed it to someone who would end up having to pass it to me anyway. My entire time at her house, she said nothing to me and made sure I knew, as far as she was concerned, that I was never there.

Immediately upon waking from the dream, the Lord told me that I (or anyone, actually) wouldn't be enough for *Undecided*, as far as his mother was concerned. At that point in his life, she wasn't ready to let him go. Conversations I had with *Undecided* after the dream were confirmations of this. A couple times, he actually said himself, "I know I'm my mama's baby. I know how much she loves me. She ain't lettin' nothin' happen to her baby."

That dream was a dream of forewarning. God was alerting me of possible, unnecessary rejection, heartache and headache.

Dream #3

This dream was a revelatory dream that became my final warning before I shut things down with *Undecided*. It was the most vivid of all the dreams I recorded throughout that year.

I was at an indoor pool. The stands were filled with people, but it wasn't because there was a swim meet going on. A final swim showcase for a swim class appeared to be the occasion. My mom was in the stands.

When the dream began, I was standing at the edge of the pool getting ready to dive, but I could feel that I had inserted myself into the showcase program at a space and time that wasn't allotted for me. I knew I shouldn't have been at the pool with all eyes on me, but there I was. Everyone in the stands was yelling, "Nooooo!" They were cupping their hands on both sides of their mouths to amplify their voices because even with the echo in the natatorium, it seemed I wasn't hearing them. I was steadily adjusting my swimming cap and posturing myself to dive. I saw my mom stand up and I could hear her voice above everyone else's. Her and everyone else's arms were flailing about in repetitive crisscross movements, signaling me not to jump. Horror spilled over their faces. They were very obviously afraid for me. I could tell they were concerned for my safety. Somehow, everyone in attendance knew the dive I was about to take would hurt me. I, on the other hand, didn't think so because I'm a swimmer. I felt my pride rise in the dream. I knew I could do it. Their warning birthed a slight pang of caution at the pit of my stomach, but my confidence overrode it.

Right before I took the dive, I looked at my mom, eye to eye from a distance. Her face was in 3D, and at that moment, her flailing arms and the words forming on her lips moved in slow motion. I turned from her gaze and plunged into the deep end of the pool. To the very bottom. Much farther down than I thought I would go.

I remember the thoughts that went through my head as I was under water and how I immediately understood why they didn't want me to jump. Of all the times I'd ever been swimming and diving in the deep end, I'd never gone down as far as it seemed I went that time. It felt like forever getting back to the surface, and the whole time I fought my way up, I wished I would've listened. I pushed at the water with every bit of my strength to propel my body to the top to prove that I wouldn't suffer the harm they anticipated. It was exhausting. I was losing steam. My chest burned. My head throbbed. My arms and legs were giving out.

When I emerged from the deep and finally took the breath I fought so hard for, no one showed any real relief for my having not drowned or hurt myself. There was an eerie stillness, and in that stillness I zeroed in on my mom's face. She just looked at me and shook her head as I struggled to tread water to get to the pool's edge.

In the next scene (yes, this is how I dream), there was a set of twins at the pool. One twin went up for the dive while the other stood on the sidelines and watched. The twin who went up for the dive experienced the exact thing I just described. The audience was yelling for him not to jump. They were crisscrossing their arms.

The same horror was on their faces. But just like me, the twin took the dive. When he came back up to the surface after having plunged down the way he had, everyone could tell something wasn't right. Lifeguards laid him on the ground to assess his well-being. He was able to talk a little, but he was certainly exhausted to the point of little to no movement of his limbs. For a minute, as he lay there, the lifeguards thought he would be fine, but no sooner than they thought all would be well, the twin's head began to swell, and shortly thereafter, he died. The other twin had stood in shock at the edge of the pool the entire time, mouth agape, watching.

Did you notice *Undecided* was nowhere in the dream? That's because in this one, God was speaking directly to me to reveal what was going on with my character as a result of my decisions. I was disobedient. My discernment was low. I was being led by my feelings rather than by my spirit. I was ignoring wise counsel. And all of this made me seem like two different people, hence the twins. Two Ianthas were operating in the one Iantha's body that was presented in the first scene of the dream. There was Twin Iantha-1 who knew better and stood and watched and said nothing while Twin Iantha-2 did everything that Twin Iantha-1 should have kept her from doing. Iantha-1 (righteousness, godliness) had a first-class ticket to watching Iantha-2 (disobedience, pride) die from her folly and it was Iantha-1's fault for not warning her.

In Scene One of the dream, the Lord wanted me to experience the emotions first. He wanted me to feel the warnings, the pride, the fear, the pain, and the concern from the onlookers, so when I saw the twin take the fall later in the dream, I could know that he was me.

My mom, the parent figure, was God, the one who knows best for me. She was warning me, but when I didn't listen, she just sat down and shook her head. She, like God, allowed me to suffer the consequences of my free-will choice.

Iantha-2's physical death was symbolic of my ignoring all sensibility and sound judgement in my situationship with *Undecided*. It was a vivid depiction of me losing myself and "drowning" in a pool of foolish decisions.

The true Iantha was almost no more. I looked like myself on the outside, but I wasn't who God was calling me to be on the inside. If I didn't heed God's warnings, I was headed for destruction.

Understanding Undecided #7 – When you belong to the Lord, He will chase you. Be grateful for that!

Let's face it. Sometimes we put ourselves in unfavorable situations. We can know it's not good for us, and we still engage. We can know it will hurt us, and we still press on. And like me in my situation with *Undecided*, we can hear directly from the Lord that we're not where we're supposed to be and stay anyway. But our God, who loves us with an everlasting love, doesn't let us stay in our mess without at least warning us that we are, in fact, in a mess. He loves us too much not to try to rescue us. By way of His Holy Spirit, He alerts us of pending danger. He speaks to us in our prayer time. He speaks to us in our dreams. He uses family and friends to speak into our lives. He uses our pastors' sermons. He sometimes uses even strangers to speak to us about our situations. Shoot, God will use anything that He knows will get our attention because He loves us too much to let us settle for love that's not like His.

God literally chased me down with warnings until the very end of my time with *Undecided*. He showed me time and time again that I wasn't where I should be. He reminded me, as often as was necessary, that I could get out. That I *should* get out. And He didn't give up on me when I ignored His warnings. He didn't turn His back on me and leave me. He showed me what I needed to know, He let me make my own choices, and when I finally saw that my choices were clearly to my own painful detriment, He comforted me and let me walk away with the lesson. He never punished me because He knew I would suffer enough from shouldering the brunt of the hurt from my own foolishness. He simply waited for me to come to my senses, and He loved me.

Are you where I was with *Undecided*? Or *Puppy Love*? Or any of the other guys mentioned in this book? Are you in a relationship that you know is unfruitful? Is the Lord sending warning after warning in your quiet time, through friends and family, and/or through your pastor's sermons? Are you hearing from Him in your dreams? Heed the warnings, my girl, because if you answered "yes" to any of these questions, you're miserable right now. I know you are. Let the Lord take care of you as only a good Father can. He knows what's best for you. He knows the path you're walking, and He sees the destruction ahead. Save yourself the unnecessary snares, headache, and heartache. He loves you. He's never stopped loving you, and His love is chasing you. Stop running *from* Him, and run *to* Him. Leave the "love" that doesn't love like God's love. Wrap yourself in the arms of your First Love.[18]

He has better for you.

---

[18] Revelation 2:2-4, *Holy Bible*

Tweet your takeaways from *Undecided*.

#HWIEUndecided

If it resonated with you,
it can probably help someone else.

Tag me in your posts on Twitter and Instagram.

Let's connect!

@ianthasinsight

A Final Word

After reading all you've read, I'm sure you're wondering if I've been in any other relationships or situationships since *Undecided*, and the answer is **No**. I have not. Throughout the years since *Undecided*, I've just been enjoying using every gift God has given me to make disciples.

Now, have there been suitors? Yes. Have there been a few dates? Sure. But what there hasn't been is what I know God has for me. I haven't seen that yet.

I'm not one of those women who has a checklist from the ceiling to the floor, and I'm not expecting perfection. I know that doesn't exist. I'm not one of those women who's sitting around waiting on my one-day husband either. I'm living and loving life, knowing that singleness is just as much a gift as marriage is.[19]

My God, it's such a beautiful gift!

What I *am* expecting, though, is to know when I know. I'm confident that when I meet him, I'll know him, and he'll know me. I've learned enough to know who he's not, so there will be no uncertainty in knowing who he is. And I won't settle. I'll remain single before I do that.

I *will* have God's best for me.

---

[19] I Corinthians 7:7, *Holy Bible*

ACKNOWLEDGEMENTS

God: My whole heart is committed to doing what You say. Your sweet Holy Spirit assured me that this book would help, encourage, challenge and free some women, so I swallowed my pride, pushed my feelings and my fear aside, and wrote what You told me to write. I don't care what it looks like; I know what it was created to do. I trust that in all of its raw transparency, it's going to do exactly what You set it out to do. Your Word assures me that because I trust in You, I will never be put to shame. And in that, I rest. I'm beyond grateful to be used by You.

Chantel: All those days and all those conversations and all those tears with *The One*…and all that side eye, and all those hard questions, and all those awkward weeks of silence trying to process what in the world was going on with me with *The Secret* and *Undecided*…Ha! I'm just grateful we can laugh about it now. I'm glad we can see that all of it was for His glory. I'm honored to have walked through it all with you, having your prayers reaching His heart on my behalf. Who else would even have enough insight to write a note to my readers? That job was yours before the foundation. In those times, all the times I traveled through in this book, you challenged me. You covered me. You loved me. And I love you.

Billisha: Who would've thought that that pledge into sisterhood would have blossomed the way it did for us? We were quite an unlikely pair, but boy am I ever grateful that unlikely doesn't mean unobtainable. I'm glad God does what He does. How would I even have gotten through this six-year tough write without you? Who else was going to push me and check in with me and be my sounding board and shoulder to cry on and literally whatever else I needed? Who else do I call when there's nothing and everything going on all at the same time? I seriously feel like you deserve a medal or a certificate of completion or something because it's been a heck of a ride. Thank you. I love you beyond the space allotted for this acknowledgement, and I'm sure you know that full well.

Bryton Entertainment: What would the book release have been without you? ***Bryan***, thank you for always encouraging me. Those texts are the best! It's an honor to call you brother. ***Denton...*** Dude... I'm convinced no one can eye a shot like you! You shall henceforth (from the day you read this) and forever be called *Angles*. And ***David***, your ability to see the big picture and pull all the small pieces together to make it work, is top notch! I thank God for our relationship, guys, and how it's grown over the years. We're now in a place where I don't even have to have it all figured out. I can simply come with an idea and the Lord uses you guys to bring the creativity and produce magic. The way you took what I envisioned and brought it to life is nothing short of incredible! I love y'all.

Video Promo Crew – Krislyn, Shagraila (Gray), Mauri, Elyssia (Le Le), DeAndre, Rodney, Jeremiah, Melvin, and Lamek: You guys blessed my socks off! For you to sacrifice the time you did to simply be there for me, I can't thank you enough. (Insert tears here) For those two days, you all were the perfect picture of what it looks like to serve for the sake of building God's kingdom. No one asked any questions beyond, *"Okay, what do you need, and how* *can I help?"* You all were just happy to serve, and I love y'all for that. I'm forever grateful to God for you.

Roundtable Readers – Asia and Tonjula: Thank you for your time and input and for experiencing that amazing pot of gumbo with me. You all told me the truth that helped me see what I couldn't see, and that gave me the last boost I needed to push to the finish. I love y'all.

Mrs. Sallie Rose Hollis (Editor): I don't know if many Journalism/Communications grads get the honor of working with their professors on personal post-graduate projects, but I'm honored and so very grateful to be able to say that I did. Talk about a full circle moment! I'm grateful for the classes I was privileged to take with you at Tech where you taught me what it means to write well. But I'm even more grateful for having you "walk alongside me" to make sure I did (except for this *Acknowledgements* section that I couldn't share with you during edits). Thank you for your time, expertise, encouragement and honesty. God knew you were who I needed. I'm already looking forward to my next visit to Ruston so we can enjoy dinner without having to talk business. And this time, we're having dessert! My treat!

Reesee (Writing Coach): You're so much more than my coach. You're my sister and friend and such a safe space for me. I'm grateful for your expertise, your honesty and your love. Thank you for pushing me to write without restraint. Your feedback on just that first section changed the game! I love you.

Hill Photography, LLC (DeeAnna): Thank you for **WOW**ing me (and the world) with the book cover photo! I mean, I had seen your work and had expectations for greatness, but I'll never forget how blown away I was when I opened that e-mail and saw all the pictures from our shoot. The cover captured exactly what I wanted to convey. You're gifted, Sis, and I thank God for you.

Mrs. Deborah and Krystal: Thank you for believing in me and seeing what God was doing with this book. ***Mrs. Deborah,*** you purchased the first book well before it was even published. I shared with you, in brief, that your seed encouraged me to push to the finish, but you may never know just how important that seed was. There were moments when getting to the finish was just downright hard, but I knew I'd already sold a book, so that's what kept me going. ***Krystal,*** you know my heart's desire to have this book in women's hands all over the world, and you, too, planted a seed by purchasing books so you could give them away to women as the Lord leads you. Blessed my socks off! I love y'all so much. Thank you!

David's Jumbo Sunflower Seeds: You are the official writing snack, and I thank you.

www.ianthasinsight.com

- "Book Talk" Sessions with Iantha
- Order *He Wasn't It Either* in bulk for your book club
- Order *Stories That Teach Girls* in bulk for your youth group
- Book Iantha to speak at your event

Made in the USA
Columbia, SC
06 September 2023

22531569R00152